INNOVATION
is the
BEST MEDICINE

The extraordinary story of Datascope

Use all your powers along lines of excellence.

— Greek, origin unknown

INNOVATION
is the
BEST MEDICINE

The extraordinary story of Datascope

Jeffrey L. Rodengen
Richard F. Hubbard

Edited by Melody Maysonet and Debra Kronowitz
Design and layout by Sandy Cruz with Tracy Moon

Write Stuff Enterprises, Inc.

1001 South Andrews Avenue, Second Floor

Fort Lauderdale, FL 33316

1-800-900-Book (1-800-900-2665)

(954) 462-6657

www.writestuffbooks.com

Copyright © 2004 by Write Stuff Enterprises, Inc. All rights reserved. No
part of this book may be reproduced or transmitted in any form by any
means, electronic or mechanical, including photocopying and recording, or
by any information storage or retrieval system, without permission in writing from the publisher.

PUBLISHER'S CATALOGING IN PUBLICATION

Rodengen, Jeffrey L.

    Innovation is the best medicine: the extraordinary story
of Datascope / Jeffrey L. Rodengen, Richard F. Hubbard;
edited by Melody Maysonet and Debra Kronowitz; design and
layout by Sandy Cruz and Tracy Moon. —
1st ed.

    p. cm.

    Includes bibliographical references and index.

    LCCN 2002115061

    ISBN 0-945903-96-0

1. Datascope (Firm) — History. 2. Medical instruments
and apparatus industry — United States — History.
I. Hubbard, Richard F. II. Maysonet, Melody.
III. Kronowitz, Debra. IV. Title.

HD9994.U54D38 2004   338.4'7681761'0973
                       QBI04-200270

Completely produced in the United States of America

10 9 8 7 6 5 4 3 2 1

ALSO BY JEFFREY L. RODENGEN

The Legend of Chris-Craft

IRON FIST:
The Lives of Carl Kiekhaefer

Evinrude-Johnson and
The Legend of OMC

Serving the Silent Service:
The Legend of Electric Boat

The Legend of
Dr Pepper/Seven-Up

The Legend of Honeywell

The Legend of Briggs & Stratton

The Legend of Ingersoll-Rand

The Legend of Stanley:
150 Years of The Stanley Works

The MicroAge Way

The Legend of Halliburton

The Legend of York International

The Legend of Nucor Corporation

The Legend of Goodyear:
The First 100 Years

The Legend of AMP

The Legend of Cessna

The Legend of VF Corporation

The Spirit of AMD

The Legend of Rowan

New Horizons:
The Story of Ashland Inc.

The History of American Standard

The Legend of Mercury Marine

The Legend of Federal-Mogul

Against the Odds:
Inter-Tel—The First 30 Years

The Legend of Pfizer

State of the Heart:
The Practical Guide to Your Heart and
Heart Surgery
with Larry W. Stephenson, M.D.

The Legend of
Worthington Industries

The Legend of IBP, Inc.

The Legend of
Trinity Industries, Inc.

The Legend of
Cornelius Vanderbilt Whitney

The Legend of Amdahl

The Legend of Litton Industries

The Legend of Gulfstream

The Legend of Bertram
with David A. Patten

The Legend of
Ritchie Bros. Auctioneers

The Legend of ALLTEL
with David A. Patten

The Yes, you can of
Invacare Corporation
with Anthony L. Wall

The Ship in the Balloon:
The Story of Boston Scientific
and the Development of
Less-Invasive Medicine

The Legend of
Day & Zimmermann

The Legend of Noble Drilling

Fifty Years of Innovation:
Kulicke & Soffa

Biomet—From Warsaw
to the World
with Richard F. Hubbard

NRA: An American Legend

The Heritage and Values
of RPM, Inc.

The Marmon Group:
The First Fifty Years

The Legend of Grainger

The Legend of
The Titan Corporation
with Richard F. Hubbard

The Legend of Discount Tire Co.
with Richard F. Hubbard

The Legend of Polaris
with Richard F. Hubbard

The Legend of La-Z-Boy
with Richard F. Hubbard

The Legend of McCarthy
with Richard F. Hubbard

InterVoice:
Twenty Years of Innovation
with Richard F. Hubbard

Jefferson-Pilot Financial:
A Century of Excellence
with Richard F. Hubbard

The Legend of HCA
with Richard F. Hubbard

The Legend of Werner Enterprises
with Richard F. Hubbard

The History of J. F. Shea Co.
with Richard F. Hubbard

True to Our Vision
with Richard F. Hubbard

The Legend of Albert Trostel & Sons
with Richard F. Hubbard

TABLE OF CONTENTS

INTRODUCTION

WHEN LARRY SAPER BUILT the first Carditron in 1964, he invented more than a revolutionary new heart monitor; he founded what would become a lasting legacy — a company called Datascope, whose success would exceed even his own youthful ambition.

It's hard to imagine that at the time the medical profession was just beginning to understand the workings of the heart and that the technology for cardiac monitoring and cardiac surgery was still in its infancy. Today angioplasty, valve replacements, and open-heart surgery are commonplace procedures in large part because of the kind of innovation on which Saper founded his company.

Saper knew from a young age that he wanted to do something important. His humble beginnings made fulfilling his dreams all the more challenging — and all the more rewarding.

When Larry's parents, Morris and Bertha Saper, immigrated to the United States in 1928, America held the promise of opportunity, but the Sapers surely could not have imagined how fully their soon-to-be-born son would realize the American dream.

Saper is multidimensional, a kind of Renaissance man driven even as a young electrical engineer by intelligence, entrepreneurial spirit, and professional and personal passions.

Motivated by the challenge of starting a company, Saper was determined to make a better heart monitor — the first with a display synchronized to heart rate. Saper's monitor was also to be considerably smaller than conventional monitors.

In 1964 he purchased a two-by-four-foot formica worktable for $20, set it up in his home, and began engineering a cardioscope prototype that would ultimately lead his company to become a major player in the medical device industry.

Once the engineering was worked out, Saper incorporated his fledgling company and rented a small office for $75 a month in a Bronx, New York, neighborhood. A dental technician named Sam Gerson had an office across from Saper, and Gerson would use his dental drills to finish the prototype.

"Dental technicians have all these marvelous little tools," Saper said. "I didn't have anything to drill these tiny holes I needed to drill. Sam was good to me. Luckily, I was able to finish the prototype with his help."

Gerson, likewise, had fond memories of Saper. "He was very energetic, very honest, and very analytical. He was always experimenting. He had all kinds of testing machines, and he was always at the office," he recalled.

Determined to create a successful business, Saper focused on what his company *should* contribute to patient care. "We make medical devices that are there to provide services to people who are sick," Saper later told his employees. "And unless you would use our products on yourself or someone you love, it's not a product that should reach the market; it's not a product that should be sold."

His business philosophy: "to make things, new things, better things." Money became a by-product of this philosophy that guided his business decisions, then and now. The key to Datascope's success — a high level of innovation.

Other innovators soon joined in Saper's vision, and together they pioneered intra-aortic balloon pump and catheter technology. More revolutionary products and discoveries for cardiac assist soon followed, and Datascope grew exponentially, becoming a publicly traded company in 1972.

By 2004, the year of its 40th anniversary, Datascope had evolved into a world-class manufacturer of unique, and often lifesaving products in interventional cardiology and radiology, anesthesiology, cardiovascular and vascular surgery, emergency medicine, and critical care.

Though Datascope has grown and changed immensely, Saper's perpetual quest for insight and his unrelenting spirit of innovation remains the cornerstones of the company's success.

"We prize innovation," he said. "The desire to innovate is a basic element of our company's character. We will work for our future growth with great energy, and for all the right reasons."

ACKNOWLEDGMENTS

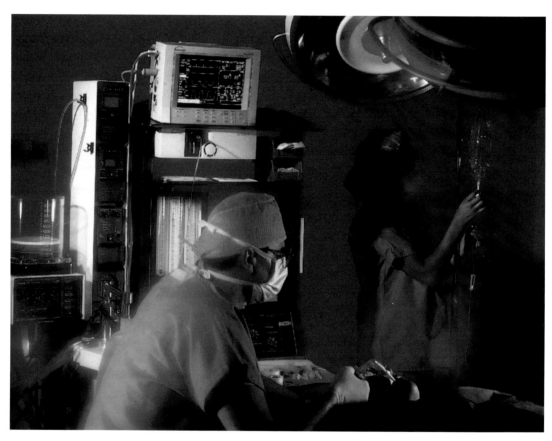

MANY DEDICATED PEOPLE ASSISTED IN the research, preparation, and publication of *Innovation is the Best Medicine — The Extraordinary Story of Datascope Corp.*

The principal research and assembly of the narrative timeline was accomplished by research assistant Donna Pulese-Murphy. Former Senior Editor Melody Maysonet, along with former Executive Editors Torey Marcus and Jon VanZile, and ultimately Senior Editor, Debra Kronowitz, oversaw the text and photos while the graphic design of Senior Art Director Sandy Cruz, along with Tracy Moon of Studio Moon, brought the story to life.

A number of key people associated with Datascope Corp. lent their efforts to the book's completion, sharing their experiences, providing valuable oversight for accuracy, and helping guide the book's development from outline to final form: Larry Saper, founder and CEO; Murray Pitkowsky senior vice president, CFO, treasurer, and secretary; Nicholas Barker, vice president of corporate design; and George Heller, board member.

Many other board members, executives, employees, retirees, and family members enriched the book by discussing their experiences. The authors extend particular gratitude to these men and women for their candid recollections and guidance: Alan B. Abramson, Fred Adelman, Carol Agnese, William Asmundson, John Benkoczy, Dr. David Bregman, Steve Block, Lisa Brishchler, John Budris, Gayle Carr, Frank Casamassina, Greg Cash, Susan Chapman, Irv Citrenbaum, Betty Clark, Jim Cooper, Anne Cuny, Gordon Dewhurst, Ron Doyle, Therese Dudek, Tom Dugan, Tanya

Fawcett, Frank Frisch, Patrick Gaude, Sam Gerson, Brett Giffin, Len Goodman, Len Gottlieb, Dr. Joseph Grayzel, Frank Gutworth, Bob Hamilton, Dotty Hanratty, George Heller, Bob Hill, Peter Hinchliffe, Deb Joseph, Walter Kaiser, Sondra Kaufman, Boris Leschinsky, Francois Lievre, Tom Lindstrand, Dennis Mattessich, John McDonough, Gary Mohr, Dr. Spyridon Moulopoulos, Pat Napoda, Martin Nussbaum, Arno Nash, Lesla Orsino, Manuela Psimitis, Phanos Psimitis, Jeff Purvin, Mark Rappaport, Susan Reilly, Dr. William Rassman, Adam Saper, Carol Saper, Gary Sagaas, Hank Scaramelli, Bob Schock, Gary Schwartz, Tim Shannon, Patricia Shields, Warren Shoop, Donald Southard, Jeff Skulsky, Susan Spadoni, Paul Southworth, Rosanne Terraciano, Bob Terranova, Bob Velebir, Noelle Walker, Jonathan Williams, and Ari Zak.

Special thanks is extended to the dedicated staff and associates at Write Stuff Enterprises, Inc.: Senior Editor Mickey Murphy; Kevin Allen, copy editor; Rachelle Donley and Dennis Shockley, art directors; Mary Aaron, transcriptionist; Barbara Koch, indexer; Bruce Borich, production manager; Marianne Roberts, vice president of administration; Sherry Hasso, bookkeeper; Kelly Chapman, executive assistant to Jeffrey L. Rodengen; and Lars Jessen, director of worldwide marketing.

Lawrence "Larry" Saper in 1959, five years before he invented the Carditron and founded the company that would become a lasting legacy.

CHAPTER ONE

A MAN WITH VISION

I came to the realization that I didn't have to invent the greatest thing in the world to go into business. All I had to do was make something better.

– Larry Saper, founder and CEO of Datascope

IN MODERN TIMES, ANGIOPLASTY, valve replacements, and open-heart surgery have become commonplace procedures, but just 50 years ago, the medical profession was still struggling to understand the workings of the heart, and the medical technology for monitoring and operating on the heart was in its infancy.

When Lawrence "Larry" Saper built the Carditron in 1964, he invented more than a revolutionary new cardioscope; he also founded what would become a lasting legacy — a company called Datascope.

Although determined to create a successful business, Larry Saper also focused on what his company should contribute to patient care. "We make medical devices that are there to provide services to people who are sick," Saper once told his employees. "And unless you would use our products on yourself or someone you love, it's not a product that should reach the market; it's not a product that should be sold."[1]

Other innovators soon joined in Saper's vision, and together they pioneered intra-aortic balloon pump and catheter technology. More revolutionary products and discoveries soon followed, and the company grew exponentially, becoming a publicly traded company in 1972. By 2004, the year of its 40th anniversary, Datascope had evolved into a world-class manufacturer of unique, and often lifesaving products in interventional cardiology and radiology, anesthesiology, cardiovascular and vascular surgery, emergency medicine, and critical care. Though Datascope had grown and changed immensely, Larry Saper's perpetual quest for insight and unrelenting spirit of innovation remained the cornerstones of the company's success.

BIG DREAMS

Larry Saper knew from a young age that he wanted to do something big. His humble beginnings made fulfilling his dreams all the more challenging — and all the more rewarding.

Larry was still in his mother's womb when his parents, Morris and Bertha Saper, immigrated to the United States from Germany in 1928 with their four-year-old son, Louis. America held the promise of opportunity, but the Sapers surely could not have imagined how fully their soon-to-be-born son would realize the American dream.

Bertha Saper and her sons, Louis (standing) and Larry, in the Bronx in 1932. Though the Saper family lived modestly and Larry grew up during the Great Depression, he said he never felt poor, but the experience did instill in him a reluctance to borrowing money.

Above: Larry and his older brother, Louis, who exposed him to the wonderful world of mathematics.

Far left: In 1928, Larry Saper's parents, Bertha and Morris, immigrated to the United States from Germany. This photo was taken while they were living in the Bronx, New York.

Inset: The Saper family in a Bronx park in 1930.

As Larry Saper explained, "My parents were not people of means, but they were people of culture. My father was a very talented man and a skilled writer. He would send articles about issues of the day to the local press, and they printed everything he submitted."[2]

Morris Saper arrived in New York City in the spring of 1928 and secured a job as a watchmaker. Larry Saper was born a few months later, in September 1928.

In late 1929, just after the start of the Great Depression, Morris Saper lost his job. He had been out of work for about a year and a half when he opened his own watch repair and jewelry shop in a tiny store in the Bronx. As Larry Saper recalled, "There was just enough room for a single counter and an aisle, and it had a little bathroom in the back."[3]

Growing up in the Bronx, Larry became interested in the way things worked while observing his father at his watchmaking trade. "I was curious about everything," Saper remembered. "So when I was five or six years old, I was taking apart watches. I wasn't putting them together, but I was taking them apart. . . . I learned to use my hands in the watchmaking business. I learned about bearings, friction, timing, balance, escapements."[4]

The Sapers were a close-knit, traditional family and lived modestly. "My mother was a very good seamstress," Saper recalled. "She would sew shirts and other clothes for us. I never felt poor because we always had enough to eat. We knew from watching movies that there were other worlds, other ways of living, but those worlds didn't exist for us."[5]

Larry Saper's older brother, Louis, wasn't much interested in the business of watchmaking but was intrigued by how things worked and was quite skilled in mathematics. Young Larry learned a great deal from his brother. Louis introduced his younger brother to complex mathematics and algebra when Larry was still a boy. As a result of this early training, he coasted through school. He was able to skip several grades in elementary school, then attended the Bronx High School of Science, where he was especially intrigued by

calculus because he could relate the concepts to applications in science. "It's not just what you learn," he explained more than five decades later. "It's how you generalize a specific experience, and it's the same thing in business."[6]

Saper graduated from high school at age 16 and enrolled in City College of New York, one of the top engineering schools in the country at that time. He did well in college, especially in physics and mathematics — important subjects for his chosen major in electrical engineering. "I liked electricity for some reason," Saper said. "There's plenty of mathematics in it, and there's plenty of physics in it. It just appealed to me."[7]

Below: Larry (front row, fourth from right) showed an interest in science at an early age. He was a member of the Science Club at the Bronx High School of Science.

Larry Saper was too young to join the military during World War II and was not yet 17 by the time the war ended in August 1945. His father died a year later, and with Louis already in the army, Larry became the breadwinner for the Saper household, running his father's store.

In 1949, when Saper graduated from City College of New York with a degree in electrical engineering, he could have taken a job with the Board of Transportation of the City of New York. "But," Saper recalled thinking, "once you go there, you never get out. I didn't want a civil service job."[8]

The young electrical engineer instead began seeking a career in the private sector. He landed an interview with Fairchild Recording, in Whitestone, Queens, New York, and bought as many audio magazines as he could get his hands on to prepare for the interview. "I told Fairchild I was really fascinated by the audio frequency field," Saper recalled. "But," he conceded, "if they were making bagels, I would have been fascinated. It had been three months of looking, and I needed a job."[9]

Saper worked at Fairchild Recording from 1949 to 1952 and developed a substantial knowledge of modula-

Above: In 1949, Larry graduated from City College of New York, where he obtained an electrical engineering degree.

Opposite: Though he was devoted to his studies, Larry Saper (standing fourth from right) also enjoyed the camaraderie of friends.

tion, audio frequencies, magnetic recording, and power supplies. After his stint at Fairchild, Saper worked in New Jersey for Bogue Electric, a defense contractor for electrical machinery and magnetic amplifiers. Saper's role grew to heading research and development (R&D) for the company's electronics lab, which was developing controls for rocket propulsion.

After he left Bogue in 1959, he joined a start-up company in Long Island, but his experience proved to be less than satisfying. Unhappy with the way the company was being run, Saper began to develop a philosophy about business. In his words, "The reason why people are in business determines the quality of the business."[10]

From Saper's perspective, money should not be the main motivation for starting a business, though he realized money's importance to sustaining the business. "You can't be an idealist," he explained. "You have to achieve an economic result. But when you say you just want to make money, you're going to conduct your business with money as the decisive, ruling parameter. Money should be the essential by-product of the business."[11]

WEIGHING OPTIONS

Saper's dissatisfaction with his employer was growing. "The company was not interested in building a company, just in selling it and getting the money," he said. "They were not in business for the right reasons — at least not what I saw as the right reasons."[12]

That company was soon sold, but Saper had options — tangible ones. The start-up company had issued stock options, which gave him the financial backing he needed to achieve his immediate goal: he would take a trip to Europe and, upon his return, start a business.

When he departed for his European vacation, the start-up company's stock was at $28. When he returned, it had fallen to $8. Saper sold the stock immediately, turning a profit of $50,000. Several months later, the stock had plummeted to pennies a share.

In 1963, before leaving for Europe, Saper didn't have a clear idea about the kind of business he wanted to start. "But the question in my mind," he said, "was what do I do? So I would think of ideas. Groucho Marx once said, 'I would never join any country club that would have me for a member.' Well, I had the commercial equivalent of that: If it was my idea, it couldn't be good enough. I was looking to invent something amazing, an objective that was simply unrealistic. So I would get an idea, then throw it away."[13]

But when he returned from his vacation, everything began to click into place. He decided to capitalize on his personal strengths in engineering and technology and explore what interested him — the medical field. Most of his work experience had been with defense systems, but he saw clinical medicine as the field of the future. "This was the time of Lyndon Johnson's Great Society. There was a lot of talk about Medicare, and I reasoned that if Medicare got passed,

Larry (right) received an award from the U.S. Air Force for electronics work he had done for a military aircraft.

there'd be a lot more money for medical devices as well as for general medical research."[14] At that time, medical devices were not regulated by the government and were most often initiated by doctors. A doctor would make the device or go to an engineer to create it, and it could be put to use immediately.

THE SEED IS PLANTED

An acquaintance of Saper's, an ophthalmologist named Jacobsen, provided the inspiration for Saper's first invention when he told Saper, "You know, why don't you make a little cardioscope that doctors could carry around in their bags?"

Saper thought Jacobsen's idea was interesting, but he was not ready to make a product until he got a better grip

on what medical device products were currently on the market. In late 1963, Saper took a trip to Atlantic City, where the Society for Clinical Investigation — an organization devoted to conducting research on new medical products for hospitalized patients — was holding a trade show featuring the latest medical electronic devices. The show held a number of exhibits, but Saper quickly gravitated to the monitoring devices. "I headed for what was familiar — electronics," Saper said. "Also the seed planted by the ophthalmologist sent me to the monitoring side."[15]

The screens of the monitors measured five inches in diameter, and Saper was struck by how large they were, for they displayed very little information considering their size. The monitors in those days, he explained, did not have electronic memories, which accounted for their size. "You had this big screen with a big power supply and a bouncing ball–kind of display that left a fading trace in its wake," Saper said.[16]

Now Saper had an idea that he considered worthy of developing. He would design a smaller, lighter cardioscope, one that did more than show an electrocardiograph signal. "I didn't ask initially who was going to use the little one," he recalled. "I didn't do the market research. The presumption was that doctors would carry it around in their bags. (I later discovered that doctors didn't carry bags anymore.) But when I came back from Atlantic City, I was determined to make a small monitor."[17]

The Atlantic City experience, Saper said, "represented a watershed because I had come to grips with reality, and I had given up the Groucho Marx syndrome. I didn't have to invent the greatest thing in the world. All I had to do was make an improvement on something, make it better."[18]

For the restless young man who wanted to invent something wonderful, this realization was the fuel he needed to begin designing the first portable cardioscope and thus blaze a new trail in the medical device industry.

Years later, Saper explained the philosophy he had adopted for his company: "We have, in the course of our history, invented some very important things. Are they massive? Are they going to rule the world? No. But they did change certain aspects of medicine in a very significant way for a whole lot of people."[19]

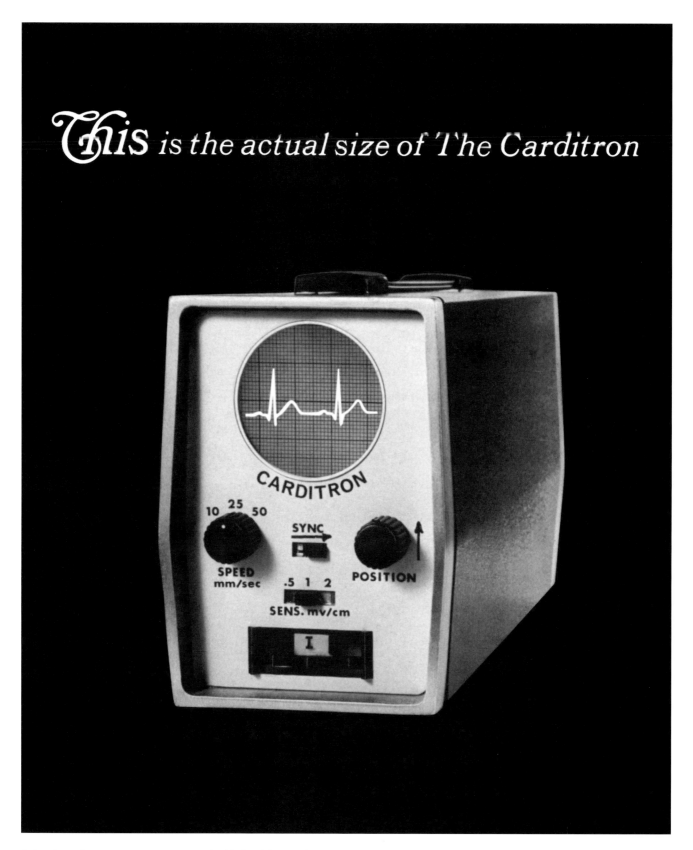

A brochure for Larry Saper's invention highlighted the Carditron's small size. The Carditron would become the first in Datascope's wide-ranging portfolio of portable, battery-operated patient monitors.

CHAPTER TWO

THE WATERSHED YEARS

1964–1970

We learn by taking an experience and examining its significance. We learn from experience by knowing, not only what happened, but why and how it happened.

– Larry Saper, 2002

S TARTING A COMPANY WOULD BE challenging for even the most enterprising person, but Larry Saper had made up his mind. He was determined to make a better cardioscope and use his invention to launch a company that would enhance patient care through technology. This was a time when clinical medicine had not yet embraced the computer revolution, when clinicians relied upon X-ray machines and electrocardiographs. Yet new technological breakthroughs were happening, and Saper wanted to be on the ground floor of what would be a revolution in patient care.

In 1964 Saper bought a two-by-four-foot formica table for $20 on which to work and set it up in his home. Then he started engineering a cardioscope prototype that would ultimately lead his company to become a major player in the medical device industry.

BUILDING THE PROTOTYPE

Once he had conceived the idea to synchronize the ECG trace to the patient's heart rate, Saper incorporated his fledgling business as Datascope. He rented a small office for $75 a month at 1831 Grand Concourse in the Bronx and began building the prototype for his invention.[1]

A dental technician named Sam Gerson had an office across the hall from Saper's and used his dental drills to finish the

prototype. "Dental technicians have all these marvelous little tools," Saper said. "I didn't have anything to drill these tiny holes I needed to drill. Sam was good to me. Luckily, I was able to finish the prototype in time with his help."[2]

Gerson, likewise, had fond memories of Saper. "He was very energetic," Gerson said, "very honest, and very analytical. He was always experimenting. He had all kinds of testing machines, and he was always at the office."[3]

Saper set himself a deadline to finish the prototype by paying $400 to book space at a March 1965 trade show presented by the Medical Society of the State of New York, an organization that strives to promote and maintain high standards of medical care in the state. "It was like a tryout for a play," Saper said. "With the $400 I'd put up, there was no way I was going to miss that deadline." Still, Saper said, "I was working until three in the morning the night before. It's like in the book *Parkinson's Law:* Work expanded to fill the available time."[4]

The Carditron was the first portable heart monitor and the first to synchronize the electrocardiogram (ECG) trace with a patient's heart rate. Larry Saper's hand holding the instrument shows its portability.

THE CARDITRON

By the start of the trade show, Saper was ready. The Carditron, as he called it, was smaller than other cardioscopes, which made it more versatile and more wieldy. It measured 9⅞ inches long, 3⅛ inches wide, and 4¼ inches high and weighed only three pounds. In short, it was a revolutionary product because it provided valuable information in such a small package. Originally created so office physicians could carry it in their bags to make house calls, it soon became popular as a portable instrument that saved valuable space in the operating room and at the patient's bedside.

Saper's Carditron gave doctors a continuous reading of heart rate irregularities. He accomplished this by creating a new method that synchronized the ECG trace with a patient's heart rate. It monitored the heart rate beat-by-beat, which provided outstanding trace clarity to more easily detect arrhythmia (alterations in the heartbeat). In sum, the Carditron was the world's first heart monitor that synchronized on a small screen the full cycle of a human heartbeat.[5]

With the Carditron, Saper had pioneered the development of compact, portable, battery-powered monitors, and in only a few years, Datascope would offer an entire line of such products. First, however, he had to make his first sale.

Larry Saper (second from left) shows off the Carditron at the Medical Society of the State of New York trade show in March 1965. Saper booked space at the show in order to give himself a deadline for finishing his invention.

VALUABLE CONNECTIONS

At the trade show, Saper met Dr. Harold Steen, chief anesthesiologist at Brooklyn Downstate Hospital, part of Kings County Hospital. "All of a sudden, a group of three or four doctors came by, and one of them did a double take," Saper remembered. "This was Dr. Steen, and he came over to my table and called the other doctors over, so they were all buzzing around this little instrument."[6]

Steen told Saper that anesthesiologists in particular would value an instrument of the Carditron's size because they often had to work within a small operating space. "An anesthesiologist sits at the head of the patient," Saper explained, "and he's got a gas machine and all sorts of cables taking up room."[7]

But if anesthesiologists were to use the Carditron, Steen explained, it would need to be explosion-proof because explosive anesthetic gases such as ether were still being used.[8]

Steen's advice proved invaluable. Saper now had a target audience for his new invention, and after some research, he was able to meet fire code regulations simply by resting the Carditron on a five-foot stand that raised it safely above any anesthetic gases that might escape into the operating room. Putting it on a stand was far superior to the more traditional method of encasing heart monitors in a thick-walled cylindrical shell.[9]

Saper made another valuable connection at the show when he met the director of medicine for Binghamton General Hospital in New York. The director showed a keen interest in the Carditron and told Saper he would be hearing from his purchasing agent.

"I was afraid to ask when," Saper said. He didn't have a secretary to field the telephone, and he worried that he might miss the call if he left the office, so he camped out in his office for several days. His tenacity paid off. Later in the week, he received a call from Binghamton Hospital's purchasing agent, who placed an order for two Model 650 Carditrons.[10]

Saper's heart was pounding as he wrote the order. "They were $465 each, so that was almost $1,000," he said. "That was a lot of money."[11]

Then the purchasing agent asked if Datascope made a heart rate alarm unit. "I was afraid to say no," Saper said, "so

An advertisement for the Monitron, a revolutionary portable, seven-pound solid-state cardiac monitor. The Monitron had a separate cardioscope, the Carditron, and a separate heart rate monitor.

I told him we did. My brother Louis actually had one in development."[12]

When the purchasing agent asked for the model number, Saper quickly replied "B," choosing a letter rather than a number because that's how plug-ins for another company's oscilloscopes were identified. The agent ordered two heart rate alarm units at about $275 apiece.[13] Later, the heart rate unit would be teamed up with the Carditron to form the Monitron, a portable seven-pound cardiac monitor.

Datascope was in business.

With his first order in hand, Saper next had to build the monitors. A friend named Alan Patricof, who later became a venture capitalist, helped him drum up investors (some of whom Saper met at the Medical Society show), who together put in $50,000 for the fledgling company. Now with enough capital, Saper browsed the Yellow Pages to find electronic parts distributors for the Carditron's components. That's how he came across the printed circuit board manufacturer that would ultimately fabricate the first 50 Carditrons Model 650.[14]

HEALTHCARE DEVELOPMENTS

The Carditron was revolutionary for its time, but it also gave Larry Saper a foothold in the area of cardiac critical care. Until the 1960s, U.S. hospitals had not established electronic monitoring for heart attack patients. Patients with chest pain and evidence of myocardial infarction (dead tissue in the middle muscular layer of the heart wall) were admitted to the hospital for supportive care, but not a lot could be done to stop the attack or minimize damage to the heart muscle.[15]

Then in 1962, Dr. Hughes Day developed the first coronary care unit (CCU) in a community hospital in Bethany, Kansas. CCUs greatly reduced the mortality rates of patients with heart problems by helping to monitor them and detect abnormalities.[16] By the 1970s, every hospital in the United States would have a critical care unit.[17]

In the meantime, however, doctors and hospitals utilized multiple small units to make a central station and used other small units that communicated information at the patient's bedside. The Carditron 650 was often one of those small units, and it would pave the way for Datascope to develop other

THE BEGINNING OF MEDICARE

MEDICARE IS A NATIONAL HEALTH insurance program for persons over 65 or individuals with serious disabilities. Enacted by Congress in 1965, it was the centerpiece of President Lyndon Johnson's "Great Society" legislative program and would have a profound effect on American healthcare.

During World War II, President Franklin D. Roosevelt had unveiled plans for a national health insurance program. After Roosevelt's death in 1945, his successor, Harry S. Truman, took the healthcare movement to the American people. Surveys showed the public was ready for such a plan, but President Truman and other proponents faced a formidable adversary determined to defeat the bill at any cost. The American Medical Association (AMA) was so opposed that it financed a national publicity campaign against the insurance plan. The AMA warned that the proposed plan would drastically lower the quality of U.S. healthcare and was also un-American: It was socialized medicine.

The AMA's campaign was successful, for it would be nearly two decades before Congress passed a national health insurance plan. By the early 1960s, however, a sharp decrease in personal income combined with increased medical needs of those who had reached retirement age and the rapidly rising cost of medical care made the need for a national health insurance plan imperative. On July 31, 1965, in Truman's hometown of Independence, Missouri, President Lyndon B. Johnson signed the Medicare bill that provided hospital and medical insurance for Americans over the age of 65, regardless of their financial means. Former President Truman watched as the bill he had championed finally became law.[1]

devices that would ultimately position it as one of the leading manufacturers of cardiac care systems.

Other events in healthcare would have a significant impact on Datascope. In the summer of 1965, for example, Congress finally passed the long-debated Medicare bill, a national health insurance program that gave millions of elderly and disabled people access to medical care. Around the same time, Congress began to address many of the perceived shortcomings regarding regulation of medical devices. Though no legislation would be passed until 1976, the mere discussion of such legislation was enough to make medical device manufacturers take notice.[18]

In addition, the National Heart Institute became actively involved in supporting heart assist system research. The institute offered grants and contracts to support applied research studies at multiple centers and in 1966 adopted a systems analysis approach to allow integration and optimization of resources from clinical centers, basic science research institutes, and the medical device industry.[19]

A WINNING TEAM

While keeping abreast of the changes in the healthcare industry, Saper hired his first employees. In its formative months, Datascope ran on a shoestring budget, but Saper had no choice but to hire a secretary who could do the administrative work and allow him to concentrate on other matters. He also hired his first sales representative, Paul Peterson, who had been working at Hewlett-Packard, but Peterson didn't stay at the company long. It was George Heller's coming on board as sales manager that proved an important turning point in Datascope's success.

In July 1965 Heller was working for Cordis Corporation, an implantable pacemaker manufacturer, when he saw Saper's advertisement in the *New York Times* seeking a sales manager. Heller was looking for new challenges in his career, so he decided to meet with Saper in his office in the Bronx.

"I liked him," Saper remembered thinking. "He seemed very solid, a man with integrity and a tremendous work ethic. He really cared about what he did. I told him, 'George, I can't afford to pay you what you're making now, but I can give you stock options, and I can promise you that I'll take good care of you.'"[20]

George Heller (left) and Larry Saper (second from left) man the Datascope booth at the 1965 American Heart Association trade show in Miami Beach, Florida.

When Saper showed Heller the Carditron, Heller remembered thinking that it was "a nice instrument. I thought it had a lot of possibilities, so I decided to give it a try."[21]

The two men shook hands, and within a week, Heller had moved into the Bronx office. Reasoning that a company as young as Datascope shouldn't be spending money on new furniture, he brought his own desk and chair from home.[22]

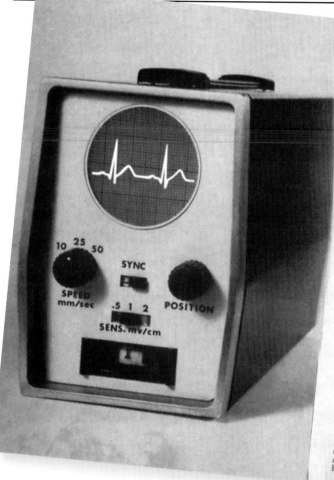

THE CARDITRON may well be the world's most advanced cardioscope. It features a standard 12 lead ECG, yet it weighs only three pounds. It makes possible extensive monitoring of the ongoing ECG—without the waste of expensive recording paper. Because it fits comfortably into a physician's instrument bag, it is as portable as a stethoscope or sphygmomanometer.

HHB-2

Carditron Unit Offers Extensive Monitoring Of Ongoing ECG

The Carditron, manufactured by the Datascope Corporation, 1831 Grand Concourse, Bronx, N. Y. 10453, offers physicians in practice and in hospitals a new capability for the clinical observation of the electrocardiogram. The Carditron cardioscope uses a proprietary method of display which has made possible, for the first time, a cardioscope weighing three pounds, with a clarity of ECG display superior to large conventional cardioscopes.

The Carditron synchronizes the ECG display with the patient's heart rate. When the heart rate is constant, the ECG shown on the Carditron display tube stays locked in position in the correct physiologic sequence starting with the P wave. The user has the option of seeing one, two or more complete cycles of the ECG.

If the patient has an arrythmia this is immediately seen on the Carditron as a movement of the ECG complex. Unlike conventional cardioscopes, there is no random shift of the ECG complex across the screen.

The Carditron is only 9⅞ inches long, 3¼ inches wide, and 4¼ inches high. Despite its modest proportions, it incorporates technical features not found in any other cardioscope in general use today. Through the use of transistors and printed circuits, miniaturization has been achieved with no sacrifice in performance. Carditron exceeds present operational standards for ECG display.

The compactness, portability and performance of the Carditron cardioscope now makes it possible to apply needed cardiac monitoring to a great many clinical procedures where the bulk of conventional equipment makes their use impractical.

The Carditron is the ideal monitor for field use such as house calls and emergencies, prolonged monitoring for the diagnosis of episodic arrythmias, an auxiliary display for conventional electrocardiograph to permit selective recording of needed data, bedside monitoring of patients, experimental research, teaching, and in hospital emergency rooms.

The second part of the story is the application of the Carditron to cardiac monitoring for intensive care, recovery room and anesthesiology. This is done by adding the Datascope Model B automatic heart rate monitor to the Carditron. Packaged in an identical module, this new unit provides the functions of heart rate meter display and automatic alarm for cardiac arrest, bradycardia and tachycardia.

It provides the unique capability of monitoring each R to R interval of the patient's ECG signal. The patient's heart rate is thus monitored beat by beat and compared with independently adjustable High and Low threshold settings. If either threshold is exceeded for longer than a preset adjustable time up to several seconds, an alarm is initiated. For maximum clinical usefulness, the preset time delay before the alarm is initiated may be set separately for the High and Low thresholds. The Type B eliminates the shock hazard associated with grounded ECG monitors.

In spite of the technical advantages of the Datascope monitoring system, the cost has been kept low. The complete cardiac monitoring system is available for less than $800.

9

"I didn't put that in the ad," Saper later joked. "Wanted: Sales manager. Must furnish own desk and chair."[23]

Heller and Saper established a marketing, sales, and product plan that put the company on a fast track toward having a worldwide presence in the medical device industry. Many elements contributed to this winning team, including their shared business philosophy and work ethic. Years after his retirement, Heller summed up his and Saper's business philosophy.

I believe there's more to working than making money. You have to make money to survive, but if money is your goal, there are much better ways to make it than through the business I was in. But if you have a passion for something, if you enjoy what you're doing, if you work to make it the best it can be, the money will follow. Larry was of the same opinion. The money follows the excellence and the passion for the products.[24]

Above: This article summarizes all the Carditron's benefits, including its "proprietary method of display that makes possible, for the first time, a cardioscope weighing only three pounds with a clarity of ECG display superior to large conventional cardioscopes."

MAKING SALES

George Heller's first challenge was to gain exposure for the Carditron and sell it to hospitals (not individual doctors as Saper had first envisioned) throughout the United States. "Doctors would never buy this," Heller remembered thinking. "I knew we had to sell it to hospitals. So how to sell it?"[25]

In these early years, Datascope could not afford to hire a direct sales force, so Heller sold Datascope's products to distributors, who then sold them to hospitals. Heller was quite successful in developing a distributor network across the United States. He started by contacting the distributors for Datascope's competitors and selling them on the quality of Datascope's products.

"Each distributor would have to buy demonstration equipment," Heller said, "so we had immediate sales. But I had to work with all the salesmen of the distributors to teach them what it was all about. A distributor salesman has a lot in his package to sell, so I was constantly fighting for his time."[26]

But, Heller admitted, the cardioscope's unique features often made for an easy sale. "You had this big tube on the competitors' thing that didn't give you any more information than a $3\frac{1}{2}$ pound scope," Heller said. "I used to put them side by side and say, 'Look at mine; look at theirs. Tell me, do you see any more in theirs than you do in mine?' And they couldn't."[27]

In addition, Heller represented the New York area himself. "That was a home base," he said, "anything I could physically cover." He also selected and attended trade shows where he could exhibit Datascope's products. "That's where we would get our good leads," he said. "Doctors would come by, and we would send the leads out to distributors. The distributor would follow up on it, or if it was local, I would follow up on it."[28]

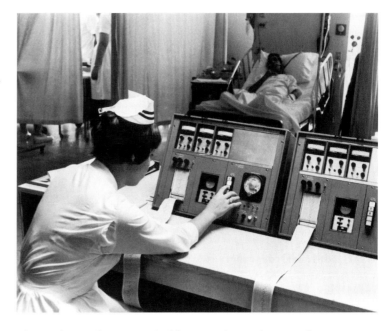

Above: The Carditron was ideal for use in hospital rooms where every inch of space was needed. At Booth Memorial Hospital in New York, a nurses station monitored as many as six cardiac patients using the Carditron.

Left: Larry Saper (second from right) and George Heller (far right) showed how the Carditron worked at a special dinner for medical professionals held in Jamaica, New York.

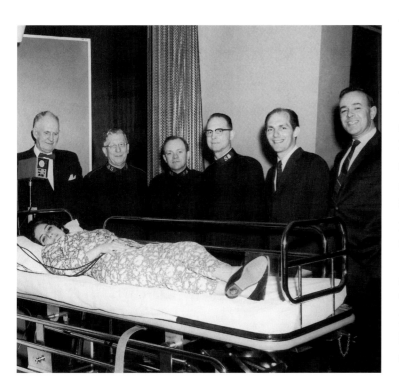

All of this was a huge amount of work for one sales manager, but Heller's perseverance and tenacity paid off.

Two key elements helped the company gain market share in the competitive patient monitoring business. First, Heller was very knowledgeable in the technical aspects of the company's product, and his easy-going temperament and enthusiasm helped gain the trust of distributors and hospitals. Second, both Saper and Heller always conducted business professionally and ethically; when they promised something, they delivered.

It was difficult for a company the size of Datascope to compete against powerhouses in the business like Sanborn, Tektronics, American Optical, Corbin Farnsworth, and Electrodyne, but Saper and Heller decided early on that the big boys would not defeat them. They would, in effect, become the figurative David in a world of Goliaths.

FORMULA FOR SUCCESS

In 1966, the Carditron's first year of production, Datascope realized $80,000 in sales.[29] Encouraged by what seemed like a triumph, Saper put more ideas into action.

He gained exposure and created an image for Datascope by recruiting Marty Stevens, then the art director for Revlon, to create the Carditron's first print advertisement. To show the Carditron's small size, the ad featured a close-up of a hand (Larry Saper's) holding the instrument. The image was accompanied by an attention-grabbing tag line that highlighted the machine's unique features: "This may well be the world's most advanced cardioscope."

Saper also found a valuable medical consultant in Dr. Joseph Grayzel, chief of cardiology at Bergen Pines Hospital, whom he met in 1967. Grayzel had invented a patented combination phono-cardiographic/apex cardiographic device. Though Saper wasn't interested in the device itself, he did like the idea that a cardiologist was developing his own medical devices. Grayzel began consulting for Datascope and joined the company's board of directors in 1969.[30]

Other early board members included George Heller, vice president for sales and corporate secretary; William Asmundson, vice president of New Court Securities; Alan Patricof, the friend who had helped Saper acquire Datascope's first investors and president of Alan Patricof Associates; and Arno Nash, Saper's high school chum who later became an international business consultant in Great Britain.

"I've been friends with Larry for a long time," said Nash. "I knew what he was hoping to do [when he wanted to start the business], and I tried very hard to encourage him because I thought the idea was excellent. We thought we were doing something that would have a real significant effect. We didn't think in terms of how much money we would make. This was not a dream. This was a hard effort to get something done."[31]

Datascope had two other rounds of financing in addition to the initial round in 1965 that raised $50,000. In 1967 the company received $147,000 from a mixture of common stock and a convertible bond, thanks in large part to Larry Tisch, who headed Loews Hotels at the time.

Two years later, Datascope sold another $110,000 worth of stock. "I wanted a much higher price for that stock issue," Saper said. "I insisted on $25, and the only one who would step up to the plate was Bill Asmundson of New Court Securities. The other investors thought the price was too high, but I held to it and he took the whole issue and made a lot of money for New Court Securities."

Saper also maintained a conservative financial plan based on Datascope being debt free. "The company has been managed very carefully so that it's consistently profitable," observed Martin Nussbaum, who began performing as outside legal counsel for Datascope in 1971. "In essence, Datascope has been able to finance its own growth."[32]

THE DATASCOPE 850

After the Carditron's success, Saper wanted to continue pioneering in physiological monitoring instrumentation and began studying the Carditron's limitations. "I'm my own worst critic," Saper said, "and I felt the Carditron was really too small."[33]

Saper's suspicions were confirmed in March 1968, when he attended a trade show presented by the American College of Cardiology. He had heard that Tektronics was entering the medical monitoring business and would be displaying its new monitor at the show. Tektronics was the defining manufacturer of oscilloscopes, and Saper was worried that this giant company would muscle in on the small market share Datascope had been able to gain with the Carditron.[34]

The Datascope 850 was the only monitor to display two vital life functions at the same time.

Even from a distance, Saper could see that Tektronics' new instrument had exceptional tooling. "I couldn't spend money on tooling," Saper said, "and that thing must have had thousands of dollars worth of tooling in the handle alone. I was afraid to go near it."[35]

Saper built up his courage to examine it more closely. That's when he realized that the instrument was also synchronized but in a very conventional and inappropriate way. He also noticed that the electrodes were the same ones he had rejected for the Carditron and that the connectors weren't durable enough for the operating room.

Even without the capital that Tektronics had, Saper was confident that Datascope could produce a superior monitor. He gave Datascope's engineer, Matt Mahoney, the instruction booklet and told him to make something better. "And he did," Saper said. "Tektronics had only one trace, and we made two. We also had far better synchronization."[36]

The Datascope 850, as it was called, was the first battery-powered monitor that simultaneously displayed two vital life functions. One trace displayed the ECG signal, and another displayed the pulse signal. It also contained a built-in alarm that sounded if the heart rate went above or below certain preset levels. The unit had a built-in battery recharger and also could be operated from line power. Shortly after this first version, Datascope added a pressure module, the Model P, which sat on top of the 850 and provided exact measurement of arterial or venous blood pressure.

Saper hired an advertising designer named David Altschiller (who later became a Datascope board member and chairman of his own ad agency, Altschiller Associates) to produce a print advertisement for the Datascope 850 and its pressure module.[37]

From the start, Altschiller and Saper were on the same wavelength about how to represent the company and its products. Altschiller said Saper made his job easier because, "unlike a lot of companies who create these 'me too' products, Larry's notion from the very beginning was to create a product that filled niches that others weren't filling. When you have a real product difference, it makes it a lot easier to advertise than when you have to be creative and try to invent something from gossamer."[38]

In addition, Altschiller said, Saper and others within the company "armed me with so much information and under-

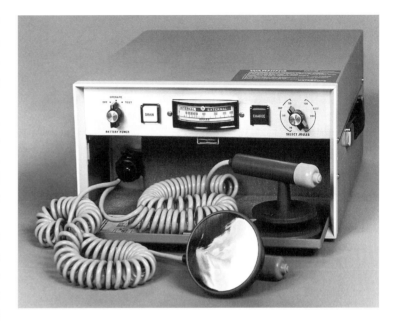

Datascope's Resuscitron defibrillator was the first battery-powered defibrillator and the lightest one on the market.

standing of the products that it's been very easy to speak in the language of the audience."[39]

Altschiller's tag line for the Datascope 850 played up how the company had improved on the Carditron. "This is our monitor outperforming all other monitors," the ad proclaimed on one page under a photo of the 850. On the facing page that showed the 850 with the pressure module on top, the ad concluded, "This is our monitor outperforming itself."

And it did. The Datascope 850 debuted in October 1970 at the annual meeting of the Society of Anesthesiology and was a huge success. "It really established an identity for us as a rising and significant player in monitoring," Saper said, noting that the 850 had launched the company into a new market area of the hospital besides the OR (operating room): post-anesthesia recovery.[40]

Not long after, in 1972, Datascope added another feature to the monitor (calling it the Datascope 860) that provided digital readouts of temperature, heart rate, and mean pressure. The Datascope 850 and 860 were so successful that within four years, the monitor business of Tektronics was sold to another company. "Our 850 did it," Saper said. "To me, Tektronics was a giant, and I learned that size didn't make a difference in our business."[41]

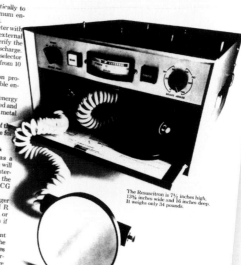
The first advertisement for the Resuscitron showed a nurse carrying it to illustrate how practical and light it was.

THE RESUSCITRON

Looking to broaden its product line into resuscitation devices, in 1970 Datascope produced a defibrillator called the Resuscitron. Fibrillation commonly follows a heart attack and involves very rapid, irregular contractions of the heart's muscle fibers. In essence, the muscle fibers of the heart are unable to pump blood and maintain circulation. Defibrillators apply a fast electrical discharge to the chest in an attempt to restore the heart's rhythm.[42]

Whereas other companies' defibrillators operated by a power line that needed to be plugged in, Datascope's defibrillator was battery powered. Because it contained a rechargeable, plug-in battery, the Resuscitron could be used anywhere and didn't have to be taken out of service to recharge. It also weighed only 34 pounds — half the weight of conventional line-powered defibrillators — and measured 7½ inches high, 13⅝ inches wide, and 16 inches deep. Moreover, it had a built-in synchronizer that produced a synchronized countershock when triggered by the Carditron ECG monitor. The Carditron monitor and battery pack could be fastened to the Resuscitron, making an all-battery-powered monitoring and resuscitation system.[43]

The Resuscitron gave Datascope another edge in the growing medical device industry. According to Dr. Joseph P. Dornich, of the Bergen County Heart Association's Pre-Coronary Care Committee, about half of all heart attack victims died before reaching the hospital, but many more would live if emergency workers could stabilize them at the scene of the heart attack.[44] For this, the Resuscitron was ideal because it was lightweight, portable, and battery powered.

Larry Saper's oldest son, Adam, who in 2001 began working for a newly formed Datascope subsidiary research firm called Genisphere, remembered a story his father told him about developing the defibrillator that illustrated one of Saper's philosophies.

In those days the company didn't have a lot of money. The two sides of the defibrillator paddles had to be glued together because it was too expensive to mold them. He had an engineer working for him – a big guy, easily stronger than my father. He was designing the paddle, and he showed it to my father. My father says, "This has got to be used in tough situations. It can't break." And my father takes it and pulls it apart. The engineer is frustrated. He works on it some more and shows it to my father again and says, "I can't pull this apart." He gives it to my father, and what happens? My father is able to pull it apart. After the third or fourth time, my father finally wasn't able to break it.

The lesson was this: You have to be your own harshest critic. The engineer could have broken it if he had wanted to break it, but there was a psychological barrier. It's very hard

to break your own work, but if you're able to bring yourself to do that rather than making getting the product out the first priority, you're going to have much better success.[45]

OFF AND RUNNING

By 1968 Datascope had grown enough to move from its sparse office in the Bronx into a 7,000-square-foot facility in Saddlebrook, New Jersey. "When Larry saw it, he said, 'We'll never be able to fill this up,'" Heller remembered. "But in no time at all, we had filled it up with production and everything else and were looking for more space."[46]

Sales were picking up too. In 1968 the company realized $180,000 in sales, and that figure grew to $380,000 in 1969 and $600,000 in 1970.[47] The next few years would prove an exciting time for Datascope. Clearly, the medical device industry was about to take off, and Datascope's creative ideas, cutting-edge technology, and devotion to quality products positioned it for exponential growth.

The System 80 was Datascope's second-generation intra-aortic balloon pumping (IABP) system. Datascope was a pioneer in the development of IABP, which used counterpulsation to assist the weakened heart and is the most effective therapy for managing cardiogenic shock.

CHAPTER THREE

BALLOON PIONEERS

1969–1971

*Whoever destroys a single life is as guilty as though he had destroyed the entire world; and
whoever rescues a single life earns as much merit as though he had rescued the entire world.*

– The Talmud

IN 1970, DATASCOPE BEGAN MANUFAC-
turing and selling one of the medical device
industry's most important products, the intra-
aortic balloon pumping (IABP) system to assist
the weakened heart. But when Datascope made
the first commercial IABP system, the therapy was
still experimental. In only a few years, however, it
would become the most effective therapy for managing cardiogenic shock and would be used widely in
patients undergoing open-heart surgery. Prior to the IABP
breakthrough, cardiogenic shock had been one of the least
manageable problems for heart surgeons and cardiologists.

EARLY BALLOON PUMPING PIONEERS

The history of intra-aortic balloon pumping can be traced
to 1958, when Dr. Dwight Harken described a way to treat left
ventricular failure with counterpulsation. Counterpulsation is a
technique that lowers blood pressure just before or during ventricular contraction of the heart (systole) and raises blood pressure during the relaxed stage of the heartbeat (diastole). In
other words, counterpulsation reduces the work load on
the heart by acting as a counterpulse. Or, as George Heller
explained, "It takes the blood out of arteries and then pushes it
back in again."[1]

Unfortunately, however, counterpulsation in those days
was, in Heller's words, "a very crude way of helping the

heart." The effect was achieved by taking blood outside of the body and pushing it back in, and this
tended to cause massive hemolysis, or disintegration
of red blood cells.

A few years later, in 1962, Dr. Spyridon
Moulopoulos, Dr. Willem J. Kolff, and Stephen
Topaz from the Cleveland Clinic published a paper
that discussed their experiments on dogs in which
they had achieved counterpulsation by inserting a
balloon pump filled with carbon dioxide into the aorta. This
"simple device," they wrote, allowed "dialostic pumping
without taking the blood outside the body."[2]

In essence, their "simple device" consisted of a catheter in
a long, narrow latex tube that was inserted into the dog's aorta,
the main artery that carries blood from the heart to branch
arteries. The tube was rhythmically inflated with carbon dioxide, and the pressure was regulated using a valve. The valve was
controlled by a timing device on the electrocardiogram so that
inflation and deflation of the balloon were correctly timed to
the animal's cardiac cycle.[3]

Moulopoulos, Topaz, and Kolff summarized their find-
ings in the May 1962 *American Heart Journal.*

Datascope offered a wide variety of intra-aortic balloon
catheters for use with its intra-aortic balloon pumping systems.

The effect of intra-aortic pumping on a failing heart is not known.... There are indications, however, that intra-aortic pumping may be of help by relieving the left ventricle of some of its work, and by increasing the blood flow and possibly the coronary blood flow during diastole....

It is hoped that the use of this device in the failing heart will result in increased diastolic blood flow, improved coronary perfusion, and decreased work for the failing left ventricle....[4]

Moulopoulos's, Topaz's, and Kolff's hope that balloon pumps could be used to help a failing human heart came close to realization a few years later. In 1967, Dr. Adrian Kantrowitz and his brother Arthur, a Ph.D. physicist and former rocket scientist, published a paper in the *Journal of the American Medical Association* reporting the first use of the intra-aortic balloon pump in three living patients. All of the patients were in shock, but they improved during the balloon pumping. One of them survived to leave the hospital.[5]

Among Kantrowitz's team was Sidney Wolvek, who designed and fabricated the surgically implantable intra-aortic balloon catheters used for Kantrowitz's research. In 1975, Wolvek would resume his groundbreaking work in IABP development as director of advanced research at Datascope.[6]

IT'S ALL ABOUT TIMING

In 1970, Dr. William Rassman, chief resident in cardiac surgery at New York Hospital-Cornell Medical Center in

THE INTRA-AORTIC BALLOON PUMP IN ACTION

THE INTRA-AORTIC BALLOON PUMP (IABP) helps the heart by increasing the flow of blood and oxygen through the heart. This is done by positioning a balloon in the aorta, the main artery that carries blood from the heart to branch arteries. The balloon reduces the workload of the heart and increases blood flow to the heart through counterpulsation. Under control of an external pump unit, the balloon increases blood pressure and coronary blood flow by inflating during diastole (the relaxed period in the heart's rhythm) and decreases

The intra-aortic balloon is guided into the aorta and inflates rhythmically to help maintain blood pressure in the heart and arterial system. It is a temporary, but very valuable, therapy for weakened hearts. *(Illustration adapted from JAMA, 8 January 1968, Vol. 3, No. 2)*

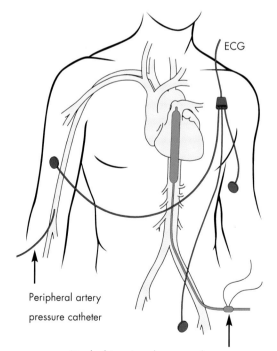

ECG

Peripheral artery pressure catheter

Attached to external pump and power source

Manhattan, saw an advertisement for the Carditron and surmised that it was ideally suited to trigger inflation and deflation of a balloon at just the right time in the cardiac cycle. He contacted Saper about using its synchronization controls to serve the strict synchronization needs for an intra-aortic balloon pumping system. Saper, who had been closely following the early experiments with counterpulsation and was fascinated by the concept, went one step further. He proposed that Datascope build the entire console for the IABP.

Saper turned to Matt Mahoney, Datascope's creative engineer who later became product planning specialist, to design Datascope's first IABP system. "Rassman had worked out the logic for the system — he taught us the logic and

physiology of the balloon pump — and Matt had a shop in his basement," said Saper. "He liked wood, so he made a nice, beautiful mahogany platform for the console and made all the electronics. He was quick, so in only three weeks, we had a balloon pump."[7]

This early system was admittedly crude, but it worked. "Nobody knew how to make balloons," said Heller. "In fact, the National Institute of Health [NIH] was issuing grants and looking for people to make them." Heller traveled the country trying to find information on how to make balloons that could be inserted inside the human body but didn't come up with many leads. "One company was making them by pouring around a Jell-O® mold and melting the Jell-O out," he said. "We made them by cutting sheets of

---

the workload of the heart by deflating during systole (the contracting period in the heart's rhythm).

The IABP system consists of a pump unit, a catheter, and an inflatable balloon. The balloon-tipped catheter is inserted into the femoral artery (near the groin) and guided into the aorta, and the catheter is attached to the external pump unit. The balloon is then inflated and deflated in sync with the heart patient's cardiac cycle.

The balloon pump is used for short-term support, usually for less than 72 hours, to help maintain blood pressure in the heart and arterial system, and is a very valuable therapy for weakened hearts. It also helps prepare patients for high-risk angioplasty/stenting procedures or drug therapy.[1]

Dr. Joseph Grayzel, a cardiologist and Datascope's longtime medical consultant, pointed out that some patients have been on the balloon pump for a week or more to let the heart recover after surgery. "These are high-risk patients," he said. "Maybe they're patients going in for non-cardiac surgery, but they have heart disease. Very often, surgeons will put the balloon in to prevent potential heart problems and have it supporting the heart while the patient is brought into the operating room. It will support them during surgery, and it will be left in after surgery for a variable period."[2]

One of the IABP's principal applications is to wean patients off the heart-lung machine (a machine used to

bypass the function of the heart and lungs) after open-heart surgery. "As you try to turn down the degree of bypass and try to let the heart gradually take over, the heart is sometimes too weak to assume that burden," explained Grayzel. "So the balloon pump is used to wean patients from the heart-lung machine over a period of several hours."[3]

In many cases, the IABP has performed miracles. Datascope board member Arno Nash witnessed such a miracle after his brother-in-law suffered a heart attack and was being treated at a hospital in Munich, Germany.

While he was in the hospital, things got even worse because a heart valve burst. They had to act fast, and he now fell into the category where you ask the doctor what his chances are and he says 10 percent. Well, that's the doctor's way of saying zero because he can't say zero to you.

Then the doctors put him on a machine – I didn't know what kind of machine it was – while they decided whether to operate. They ended up operating the following Monday, and it was successful. He came through.

On the day after the operation, the doctors told my wife and I that without the machine, my brother-in-law would be dead. So I asked them what the machine was, and they pointed it out to me in the corner. It was a Datascope balloon pump.[4]

polyurethane and gluing the edges together and then tying it with suture material. That was a balloon."[8]

Dr. Joseph Grayzel explained why the intra-aortic balloon was not elastic. "It's not like a latex or a rubber that expands," he said. "It's a fixed envelope that is simply collapsed. It's blown up to a fixed volume, and it inflates easily because there is no resistance. Nothing is being stretched."[9]

Grayzel also explained why pioneers in intra-aortic balloon pumping chose carbon dioxide (CO_2) to inflate the balloon but later switched to helium.

In the early days, when systems and balloons perhaps were not as reliable, CO_2 was a safer gas because it could be dissolved in blood without any harm. Helium, which is used today, is not nearly as soluble and runs the risk of bubbling out. But the speed with which the gas will flow through the little catheter tube to the balloon, which is in the body, depends on the viscosity of the gas. The lower the molecular weight of the gas, the lower the viscosity and the faster it will move. Carbon dioxide has a molecular weight of 44. Helium has a molecular weight of two, so you can pump it into the balloon and withdraw it faster than carbon dioxide.[10]

Datascope's first IABP system, called Cardiac Assist Control Unit 3500, was capable of copulsation (squeezing the heart), another experimental technique, in addition to counterpulsation. But the copulsating feature was confusing, Saper said, and the company soon dropped it.

Still using the polyurethane balloon, Datascope conducted the first clinical use of its IABP system at North Shore Hospital in Long Island, New York, on a patient with a failing heart. Unfortunately, the patient died a few hours after surgery, but as Saper noted, "They used the balloon as a last resort. He had no heart left to assist." For the long term, Saper was not too discouraged, for the procedure had set the stage for Datascope to make a major contribution in the area of cardiac assist.[11]

EARLY SUCCESS STORIES

Not long after, Saper and Heller were at a trade show exhibiting the balloon pump when they met Dr. David Bregman, who, together with Dr. Robert Goetz, a cardio-

vascular surgeon, had developed a refined unidirectional dual-chambered balloon designed to produce more coronary blood flow than a single-chambered balloon.

Bregman remembered how the idea for the balloon took root and how he first heard about Datascope. In 1969, he was a captain in the U.S. Air Force and a surgical resident at the Cardiovascular Surgical Research Library of Albert Einstein College of Medicine and Bronx Municipal Hospital Center. He was working under Dr. Goetz, who had gained international attention for his work on blood circulation.

Bregman had been interested in the concept of arterial counterpulsation and had read about the research done by Moulopoulos, Kolff, and Topaz. "I knew I wanted to be involved in this whole concept," he said. "I started experimenting in animals with toy balloons, and I heard that Dr. William Rassman was working with a company that was experimenting with balloons."[12]

Bregman called Rassman and found out that the name of the company was Datascope and that it operated out of nearby Saddlebrook, New Jersey. "I acquired a real premature piece of equipment from Datascope, and through this, I made something called the safety chamber, which is now an integral part of the balloon pump," Bregman said.[13]

Bregman filled a cigar-shaped balloon (a predecessor to the unidirectional dual-chambered balloon) with carbon dioxide, which moved in and out of the balloon inside the body while outside the body was a safety chamber with another balloon on it. "When you squeezed the balloon on the outside, it pushed the gas in, but it would come out again so that the gas kept moving in and out," Bregman explained.[14]

Bregman made the safety chamber by hand and attached it to the piece of equipment he had procured from Datascope. "Then I found a vacuum cleaner in the basement of Albert Einstein that I used for suction on the safety chamber to open the balloon up and fill it."[15]

By November 1969, Bregman's invention was ready. He painted the safety chamber and contacted the chief resident at Albert Einstein. "I couldn't explain it all to him," Bregman said. "I didn't even know myself what it was. I knew it seemed to work in dogs."[16]

Bregman's first patient was a gentleman in his fifties who had suffered 10 cardiac arrests. So desperate was the man's

Above: Dr. Robert Goetz coinvented the unidirectional dual-chambered balloon, which was superior to all previous intra-aortic balloons. Datascope used the dual-chambered balloon with its IABP System 80.

Right: This illustration shows how Datascope's System 80 intra-aortic balloon pump helps increase blood flow to the patient's heart.

situation that Bregman had to transport the safety chamber to the hospital via ambulance, and the paint on it was still wet.[17]

Bregman surgically inserted the balloon through the patient's femoral artery (the chief artery of the thigh, near the groin), "and within five minutes the guy was awake and asking for a beer," Bregman said. The man survived, and Bregman used his invention on three other patients within the next few months, all of whom survived an otherwise fatal condition.[18]

THE RIGHT BALLOON

In 1970, Bregman met Larry Saper and George Heller at the trade show where they were exhibiting Datascope's IABP. "We made a marriage of sorts," said Bregman. "After all, I had borrowed their machine to make the safety chamber."[19]

Saper remembered the visit he and Heller made to Albert Einstein to see Bregman's dual-chambered balloon.

We went into Bregman's and Goetz's lab, and the place where the balloons are was covered with sheets so we couldn't see them. Bregman had been experimenting on a goat, and the goat was dying, and he was exasperated. So he was pounding on the chest of the goat and trying to keep the goat alive.[20]

After Saper and Heller had signed a confidentiality agreement, Bregman and Goetz showed them the balloon, which was made with glass molds from polyurethane and miscellaneous material from the Albert Einstein laboratory.

"Goetz and Bregman showed us their secret," said Heller. "For that time, their method for making balloons was very elegant, and their balloon was very unique. They not only made a balloon; they made what's known as a double balloon. It was a balloon with another balloon on top. The little balloon on the bottom blew up first, so it acted as a valve, and the other balloon could push blood in only one direction, towards the heart."[21]

Dr. Goetz agreed to let Datascope license the balloon technology and make the unidirectional dual-chambered

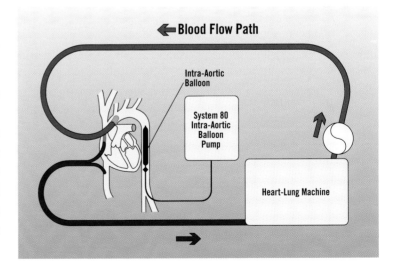

balloons for Datascope's System 80, the company's second-generation IABP system, which Datascope introduced in September 1971.[22]

"We used part of Bregman's and Goetz's method to make our own balloons," said Heller. "Then we gradually improved upon them, and the NIH said we probably had the finest balloon at that time."[23]

In the meantime, Dr. Bregman in 1970 had demonstrated that the IABP system could be used post-operatively to help the repaired heart regain normal function. In the IABP's early days, this would be its main application.

HERE AND ABROAD

Now Datascope's most immediate challenge was to sell the IABP system. "We showed it at all the thoracic and cardiovascular shows," said Heller, "and [heart surgery pioneers] like Michael DeBakey and Denton Cooley were looking at it. But our dealers weren't selling the balloon pump because it required a lot of effort."[24]

Selling such a revolutionary product was a monumental task, for surgeons had to be trained to use the new technology. Heller would demonstrate the procedure on animals, and that task alone took several hours. In addition, special balloons had to be custom-built for procedures on dogs or pigs.[25]

Furthermore, as one account later noted, "The medical establishment's early response to IABP ranged from guarded enthusiasm to incredulity.... Despite the burgeoning literature on the benefits of timely IABP intervention with human subjects, Heller found that most hospitals viewed IABP as a therapy of last resort. Often, by the time he was called to assist in a procedure the only intervention possible was divine."[26]

Another potential selling obstacle involved how the balloon was implanted. "In the original days it was done by a surgical cut-down," explained Dr. Joseph Grayzel. "That was one of the impediments to the development of the field — the fact that the cardiologist or even other surgeons would have to call a vascular surgeon to come in and place this device in the femoral artery because the technique involved sewing a synthetic graft onto the side of the vessel so you'd have a side channel into which the balloon was put. The balloon was not put directly into the artery."[27]

In 1971, Heller hired a sales manager and some other sales people to sell Datascope's monitors and defibrillators in the United States. The company also added 15 distributor sales outlets for a total of 87 throughout the United States and Canada.[28]

In addition, Heller began looking for countries outside of North America where he thought the balloon pumps would be accepted. Both he and Saper had been searching for overseas dealers, but it wasn't until early 1971 that a Dutchman named Ernst Janzen contacted Datascope from Sweden because he wanted to sell the Carditron. "Janzen had fallen in love with our cardioscope and would rather sell it over his other products," said Heller. "So Larry told him, 'Well, why don't you come to work for us and we'll start a European company.'"[29]

In 1971, Datascope started two wholly owned foreign subsidiaries: Datascope AB in Skarholmen, Sweden, and Datascope B.V. in Hoevelaken, Holland, to sell the company's products in Europe. (In 1973, Datascope would dissolve Datascope AB, but Datascope B.V. became the core of the company's European operations.)

The Medical Society of the State of New York awarded this certificate to Drs. Bregman and Goetz for their groundbreaking development of the dual-chambered intra-aortic balloon.

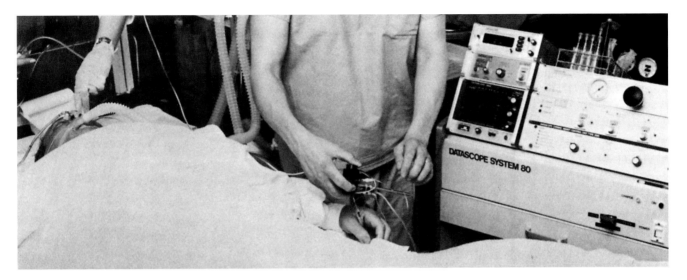

Appointed vice president for sales, Heller took on the monumental task of selling the IABP systems to surgeons throughout the United States, and Janzen, as managing director, sold them in Europe. The intra-aortic balloon pumping system sold increasingly well overseas, particularly in countries like Holland, where it did exceptionally well, Heller said, and in France and Italy, which had a greater availability of capital and a greater acceptance for the device.[30]

Despite certain challenges, no one could deny that the IABP system was a groundbreaking development in cardiac care. Though the heart still had to do some of the work, the balloon pump was capable of doing about 20 percent of the heart's work and often made the difference between life and death.[31] Very soon, other, larger companies created their own IABP systems, leaving Datascope with only about 25 percent market share. This would change after 1979, when Datascope developed the percutaneous IAB, but for now Saper was happy to contribute to the making of this important cardiac assist device.[32]

UNLIMITED OPPORTUNITIES

By 1971, Datascope had become a rising and important maker of medical devices. Datascope's main market was still the OR, but with the IABP System 80, the Resuscitron defibrilla-

Datascope's IABP System 80 saved many people's lives by rhythmically inflating a balloon within the aorta, thus reducing the workload of the weakened heart through counterpulsation.

tor, and the Datascope 850 Monitor, the company had gained a foothold in three growing medical markets: anesthesiology, emergency medicine, and cardiovascular surgery.[33]

In these early and experimentally progressive years of Datascope's history, the company was free to explore the development of new products with no governmental boundaries. But the years ahead would prove more challenging as the government began regulating the medical device industry to help assure that only safe devices would reach the market.[34]

In the meantime, however, Datascope was doing quite well. Not only was it producing innovative products that helped save lives; it was also achieving financial success, which positioned it to produce even more great products. In 1971, the year Datascope introduced the IABP System 80, the company broke the $1 million milestone, achieving $1.1 million in sales.[35] But that figure would seem small compared to what was to come during the next decade, and the products Datascope had produced — though remarkable in their own right — would seem minor accomplishments in comparison to future achievements.

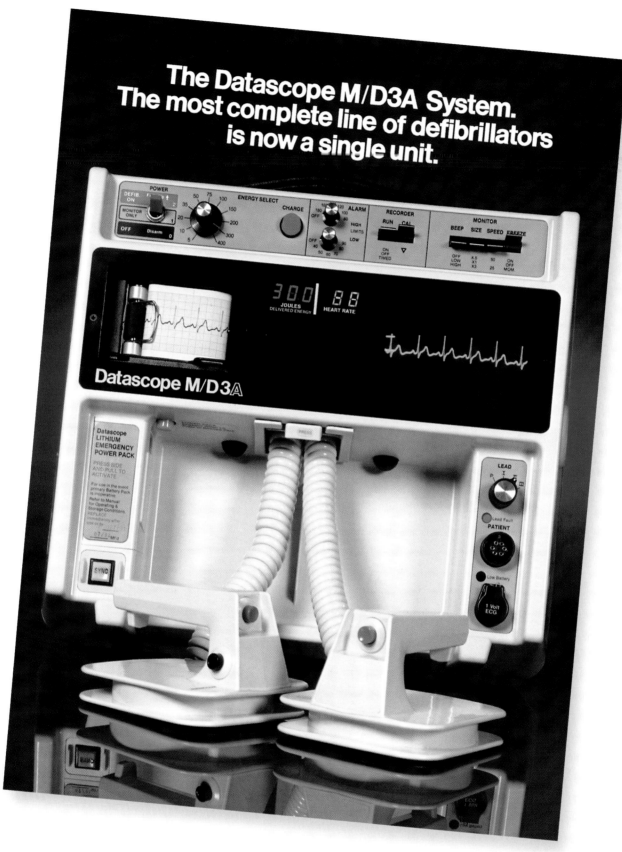

Datascope was a major innovator in the defibrillator market throughout the 1970s. The M/D3A represented the state of the art in defibrillator technology in the late 1970s.

CHAPTER FOUR

PERSISTENT INNOVATION

1972–1979

He that will not apply new remedies must expect new evils; for time is the greatest innovator.

— Francis Bacon, "Of Innovations"

THE DECADE OF THE SEVEN-
ties presented difficult challenges to
the American economy and businesses.
The beginnings of the Watergate scandal, the
growing conflict in Vietnam, and the often vio-
lent opposition to the civil rights movement had
already soured the country's mood. Then in 1973,
Egypt and Syria launched a massive offensive against Israel.[1]

Following weeks of desperate fighting, the United States
airlifted $2 billion in aid to Israel to counter the Soviet Union's
support of the Arab nations. Incensed, the Organization of Petroleum Exporting Countries (OPEC) united behind Saudi Arabia
on October 20, 1973, in a complete embargo of oil shipments
to the United States.[2]

The resulting energy crisis forced conservation to the top of
the national agenda, and the economy tossed and turned in a swirl
of inflation and recession.[3] From 1973 to 1974, consumer prices
rose 12.2 percent and continued to rise until 1978.[4]

GOING PUBLIC

Despite the floundering economy, Datascope prospered.
The year 1972 was a particularly good one, for not only did its
revenue more than double from the prior fiscal year, reaching
$2.2 million in sales; Datascope also, on April 26, 1972, became
a publicly traded company on Nasdaq. In its initial public offering, Datascope sold 105,850 shares and realized $800,000

after expenses, a small portion of which went
to pay down short-term bank debt.[5]

Datascope's decision to go public would
prove fortuitous, not only from a financial standpoint, but also because it gave Datascope "a
greater degree of visibility in the marketplace,"
according to Martin Nussbaum, the company's
outside general counsel, who worked on Datascope's initial
public offering. "Accessing the marketplace for capital was not,
in my estimation, critical to the company's growth and success
because it didn't really need that much capital from outside
sources," he said. "But clearly Datascope reached a certain watershed when it became a public company."[6]

Going public, Nussbaum said, also changed the nature of
Datascope's operations since it now had to report to shareholders
and comply with regulations of the Securities and Exchange
Commission. But Nussbaum was quick to point out that
Datascope had adhered to the ideals of corporate governance long
before such compliance became essential or even fashionable.

By the time the company went public, Saper had outlined two goals: He wanted to continue to produce innovative
products, and he wanted to build a sales force to bring those

This graphic, which appeared in several early annual reports,
represented Datascope's intra-aortic balloon pumping segment.

products to market. He was successful on both accounts. By the early 1970s, Datascope — now that it had a variety of products — had reorganized into three main product groups: monitor/defibrillator systems, physiological monitoring instruments, and cardiac assist products. Throughout the 1970s, each of these groups grew by leaps and bounds, not only in sales, but also in product innovations.

MONITOR/DEFIBRILLATOR SYSTEMS

After introducing its first defibrillator in 1970, in 1973 Datascope introduced the M/D2, a combination monitor/defibrillator designed to both identify and treat life-threatening heart rhythms. Previously, most of the company's defibrillators and monitors had been sold to hospitals, but by the early 1970s, several states, following the lead of the Los Angeles County Fire Department's Emergency Rescue Program, began training paramedics to provide emergency intensive care before a patient even reached the hospital. The portable, battery-powered M/D2 was ideal. After a patient was treated by the defibrillator portion of the unit, he or she could be monitored to verify that the therapy was successful and could be diagnosed for recurrent fibrillation.[7]

The same year Datascope introduced the M/D2, the American Heart Association (AHA) reported that half the 670,000 Americans who died of heart attacks the year before did not die in the hospital. The AHA suggested that fewer would die if more mobile coronary care facilities were capable of treating patients at the scene or in the ambulance. In addition, Dr. James Warren, former president of the American Medical Association, observed that stepped-up emergency rescue care units would save about 1,000 heart attack victims each year.[8]

This dramatic, unstaged photo shows Datascope's emergency medical devices in action.

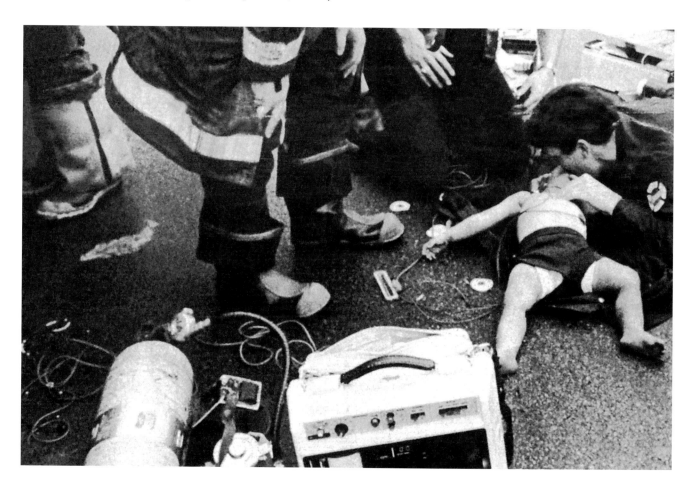

Throughout the 1970s, hospitals worked to expand and improve their emergency facilities, and paramedic rescue programs became more prevalent. By 1974, emergency healthcare equipment had become Datascope's fastest-growing product segment.[9] Late that year, Datascope increased the M/D2's appeal by introducing the Model 790 Recorder, an optional, battery-powered recorder companion to the M/D2.[10]

Then in 1975, medical studies showed that "the success rate for defibrillation of human adults is only about 65% with defibrillators which deliver 300 watt-seconds of energy...[and] the probability of defibrillating a subject who weighs over 220 pounds is extremely low." Thus, the studies concluded, "virtually all defibrillators now in use have inadequate output to defibrillate many human adults."[11]

In response to these troubling statistics, in 1976 Datascope introduced the next-generation monitor/defibrillator, the M/D2J, which could discharge 40 percent more energy than the M/D2 and most other battery-powered defibrillators. Moreover, the M/D2J was the only defibrillator that could read the amount of electrical current delivered to the patient during defibrillation.[12]

The M/D2 and M/D2J could be enhanced by the Databank, another Datascope invention, which debuted in 1976. The Databank was the first cassette recording system in emergency medicine. It recorded ECG, eliminating the need for unwieldy paper recording, as well as voice so that a caregiver's comments about the patient could be documented.[13]

In 1977, Datascope's monitor/defibrillator made headlines after the company loaned it to the Grand Mound Fire Department, of Thurston County, Washington. The only equipment the fire department's rescue unit needed to perform Medic I–type emergency service was a monitor/defibrillator system to deal with heart problems, and Datascope loaned it a system until it could finance the purchase on its own.[14]

Before the end of the decade, Datascope made one more product innovation in monitor/defibrillator systems. The M/D3 integrated a non-fade monitor, defibrillator, and strip-chart recorder in a portable package that weighed only 25 pounds. It allowed caregivers to identify, treat, and document fibrillation with one product. In addition, the M/D3 incorporated a unique lithium power source that had a five-year life and served as an emergency backup power source for the rechargeable batteries.[15]

"We really hit the mark with our defibrillator products during this time," said Mark Rappaport, who joined Datascope

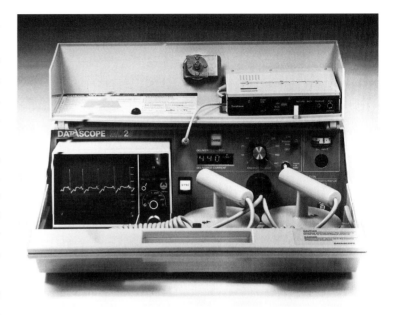

When hospitals called for smaller, more portable cardiac assist devices to equip ambulances, Datascope answered the need. The M/D2 combination monitor/defibrillator could both identify and treat life-threatening heart malfunctions.

in 1977 as a technician for defibrillators and later became director of service operations for the Patient Monitoring division. "In fact, the television show *Emergency*, an MGM production, used our defibrillators on the show. We used to modify the product for MGM so that it was a real working unit. It would discharge internally instead of to the patient."[16]

PHYSIOLOGICAL MONITORING INSTRUMENTS

In late 1971, Datascope introduced its next generation of monitoring instruments, the Datascope 860. It, like the Datascope 850, was compact, portable, and battery powered, but it also provided a digital readout of temperature, heart rate, and mean pressure in addition to simultaneously displaying the patient's ECG signal and plethysmograph signal.[17] The Datascope 860 was well received in anesthesiology and operating rooms, for it could be used to monitor patients during surgery, in the recovery room, and while transporting them from one clinical service to another. It was also a modular component of Datascope's intra-aortic balloon pump system.[18]

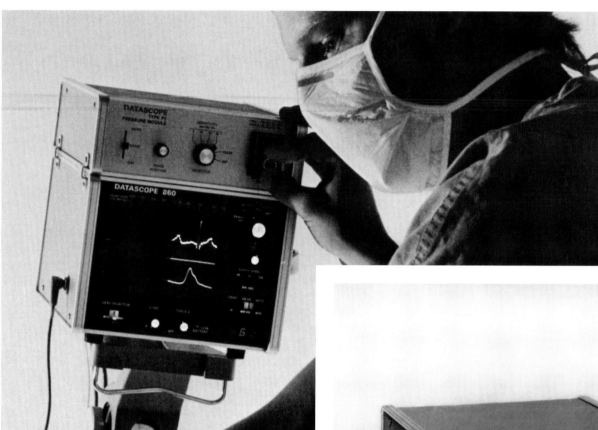

Datascope showed its technical leadership in the portable physiological monitoring market by introducing a cascade of ever more sophisticated monitors throughout the decade. The Datascope 990, a six-pound, battery-powered ECG monitor developed for the M/D2, came out in 1972 and featured a non-fade display, a trace that could be frozen, and digital readout of heart rate.[19] In 1975, the company introduced the Model 800, a new module for all Datascope monitors that was equipped with an alarm, plus a battery charger for the 990 that allowed it to recharge while in use.[20]

The Datascope 870, another non-fade, dual-trace portable monitor, premiered in 1977. Until the Datascope 870, monitors with non-fade trace display, though more effective than monitors with traces that faded, had not been widely accepted because they were too costly, too heavy, and had too short a battery operating time. But the 870 monitor had none of those disadvantages. It could perform twice as long as monitors that

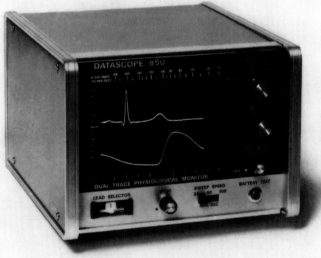

This is our monitor outperforming all other monitors.

Introducing the Datascope 850. Our Monitor. It's the only monitor in the world that is battery powered, and allows you to monitor 2 traces. (Your patient's ECG and pulse waveform.) And because our monitor consumes less power, the batteries operate for 10 to 13 hours before you need to recharge.

Our monitor also offers you a more effective method of monitoring. Beat-by-beat synchronized display.* You see one complete ECG complex in each sweep of the trace. And, at the point on the screen where the sweep ends, you can read your patient's heart rate from a calibrated scale.

Our monitor also has the fastest recovery time if you have to defibrillate your patient. The ECG returns on screen in 1 second or less.

Our monitor is also compact and weighs a highly portable 10½ lbs. Which means that your patient can be monitored from surgery to recovery room, or anywhere enroute. Without a struggle.

Now that we've told you how our monitor outperforms all other monitors, we'd like to tell you how it outperforms itself:

The Datascope 850.

*U.S. Patent #3,347,452

faded, weighed only 11 pounds, and cost no more than conventional monitors. The 870 monitor could monitor ECG, blood pressure or pulse, and temperature, making it more versatile than competitors' models. It also allowed blood pressure to be read more quickly and more accurately than other monitors could.[21]

Also in 1977, Datascope released the P3 Pressure Module, an optional companion to the 870 monitor. The P3 allowed healthcare workers to precisely monitor systolic and diastolic pressure simultaneously.[22] And at the end of the year, Datascope announced two more product developments: the 871 monitor, a lower-priced version of the 870, and the 740 recorder, a dual-channel physiological recorder companion for the 870

monitor.[23] In addition, in 1979, Datascope introduced the ESIS module, which virtually eliminated RF interference from the ECG monitor, thus displaying a signal that was easier to read.[24]

Because continuous monitoring of vital signs was playing an increasing role during surgery, while transporting patients, and in recovery rooms, demand for Datascope's mobile patient monitors grew. What's more, hospitals and doctors were requiring monitoring of more physiological parameters, and Datascope's monitors covered the gamut, from ECG, heart rate, and pulse waveform to blood pressure and temperature. By 1977, Datascope, which had pioneered the development of compact, portable, battery-powered monitors, had become a leading manufacturer of battery-powered monitors for surgical, recovery room, and mobile patient monitoring.[25]

CARDIAC ASSIST

In 1971, when Datascope introduced the System 80 intra-aortic balloon pumping system with the exclusive (later patented) dual-chambered balloon, counterpulsation therapy for the heart was still experimental. Year by year, however, the therapy gained wider clinical acceptance as the best treatment for cardiogenic shock and as temporary assistance to the heart before and after open-heart surgery or revascularization procedures (surgery to provide blood to a body part or organ). Only a few years after its introduction, sales of the System 80 and the disposable intra-aortic balloons (which Datascope began offering in individually wrapped sterile packs in 1973) increased sharply, climbing from $261,000 in 1972 to $620,000 in 1973. And as more hospitals recognized the IABP system's value and users became

This is our monitor outperforming itself.

We've developed the Type P Pressure Module to make the Datascope 850 outperform itself. Now, our monitor can also measure arterial and venous blood pressure (or any physiological pressure for that matter).

Turn the Pressure Module on and the lower trace on the screen (normally the pulse trace) becomes 2 traces: a pressure waveform and a pressure reference line.

Turn a dial and you can adjust the reference line to intersect the pressure waveform anywhere you want a measurement. Then simply read the pressure on the reference dial — digitally.

Call us at area code 201-845-7650. Or write to Datascope Corporation, 520 Victor Street, Saddle Brook, New Jersey 07662. We'll be happy to give you additional information on the Datascope 850 and the Type P Pressure Module.

We don't think you should have a monitor that merely performs, when you can have one that outperforms.

The Datascope 850. with Pressure Module.

In 1964, Datascope had pioneered compact, portable, and modular monitoring instruments with the Carditron, and the company continued offering ever more sophisticated models. The battery-powered Datascope 860 (opposite, far left) monitored temperature, heart rate, and mean blood pressure and displayed the patient's ECG and plethysmograph signals. The Datascope 850 with pressure module (left) "outperformed itself" by measuring arterial and venous blood pressure. With the pressure module, the pulse trace became two traces: a pressure waveform and a pressure reference line.

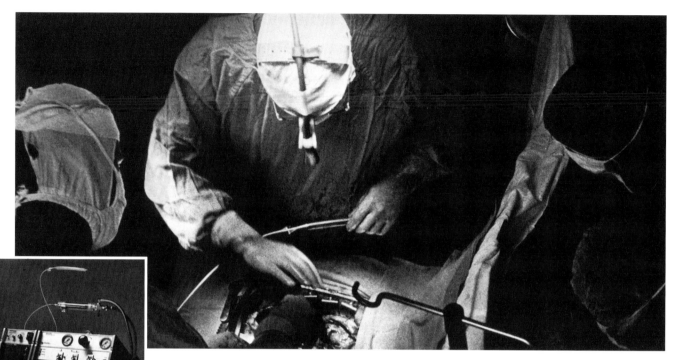

more experienced with it, sales continued to ratchet upward.

A surgeon prepares to insert Datascope's dual-chambered intra-aortic balloon (above), which is attached to the IABP System 80 (left). The balloon will rhythmically inflate and deflate in the patient's aorta, taking the workload off the heart and thus giving it a chance to recover.

Datascope made another pioneering innovation in 1974, when it introduced the first pediatric-size balloon in response to a growing number of surgical applications in children.[26] (Datascope would develop a more effective pediatric balloon catheter in the early 1980s.) A year later, the company stepped up its education and training efforts by publishing an IABP newsletter and holding the first IABP User Training Clinic. That year also marked the first clinical symposium on the Datascope IABP system.[27] Clinical training would become one of Datascope's hallmarks in later years.

By 1976, the intra-aortic balloon pumping systems had become Datascope's fastest-growing product group, with sales increasing 76 percent over the previous year to $1.8 million.[28]

Also in 1976, Datascope introduced another ground-breaking cardiac assist product: the Pulsatile Assist Device (PAD). After being inserted into the arterial line of a heart-lung machine, this disposable device could be used during open-heart surgery to convert the constant blood flow from a heart-lung machine so that it emulated the body's natural, pulsating flow. Such pulsatile perfusion was better for the body's organs and circulation than the steady flow provided by heart-lung machines. In addition, the PAD could be synchronized with the heartbeat to produce pulsation or counterpulsation. But unlike intra-aortic balloons, the PAD was noninvasive; it was the first device to produce pulsation and counterpulsation from the heart-lung machine without additional surgery. In clinical studies, the PAD was shown to be especially helpful in reducing mortality rates and complications in patients undergoing open-heart surgery.[29]

One of the first uses of the PAD was performed by Dr. David Bregman, assistant professor of surgery at Columbia-Presbyterian Medical Center in New York and the cocreator of the first successful dual-chambered intra-aortic balloon. Bregman used the PAD in 100 clinical trials on open-heart surgery patients and reported that all the

Myocardial Infarction Rate Lowered

Says New Pulsatile Assist Device Reduces Open Heart Surgery Risk

A new heart assist device that provides the benefits of intra-aortic balloon pumping without requiring that a balloon actually be threaded into the patient's aorta has drastically reduced the risk of open heart surgery.

Reporting on the noninvasive pulsatile assist device (PAD), David Bregman, M.D., of the Columbia-Presbyterian Medical Center, New York, outlined his success in substantially lowering the rate of perioperative myocardial infarctions among the first 100 open heart patients to be perfused by a heart lung machine with an online PAD. He explained that 73 of 100 patients assisted were either New York Heart Association class III or IV or had ejection fractions of less than .3.

"The majority of the procedures were multiple coronary artery grafting but several other procedures were performed including ventricular aneurysms and combined valve coronary and valve aneurysm procedures," said Dr. Bregman, who is Assistant Professor of Surgery at the Columbia-Presbyterian Medical Center.

"All of the patients assisted with the pulsatile assist device were successfully weaned from the heart lung machine. Only one patient in the entire group required intra-aortic balloon pumping a few hours after the completion of his operation. This was the only patient in the group who sustained an acute intraoperative myocardial infarction, and this patient survived after five days of intra-aortic balloon pumping."

In general, Dr. Bregman pointed out, the pulsated patients have appeared to have
(Continued on page two)

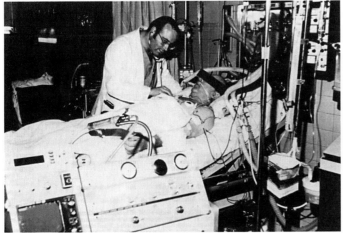

Dr. David Bregman is seen administering new heart assist device.

patients except one were successfully weaned from the heart-lung machine. He also said that the pulsated patients appeared to have done better than their counterparts who were not pulsated. Bregman concluded that the PAD was a safe and reliable pulsatile assist device to enhance intra-aortic balloon pumping.[30]

As with the IABP system, widespread clinical acceptance of the PAD did not come immediately. But users of the PAD reported favorable results, and additional clinical studies at medical institutions repeatedly showed that the PAD was a valuable cardiac assist product.[31]

Also in 1978, Datascope began selling the System 82, its third-generation IABP system, which featured the non-fade 870 Monitor with electro-surgical interference suppression (ESIS) and was easier to operate than the System 80.[32]

One of the first uses of Datascope's PAD, a pulsatile assist device (below), was performed by Dr. David Bregman (left), who was successful in weaning high-risk cardiac patients from a heart-lung machine. The PAD could also eliminate the need for preoperative IABP.

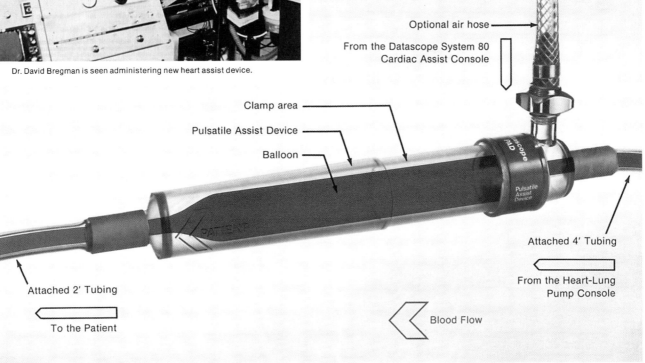

Optional air hose

From the Datascope System 80 Cardiac Assist Console

Clamp area

Pulsatile Assist Device

Balloon

Attached 4' Tubing

From the Heart-Lung Pump Console

Attached 2' Tubing

To the Patient

Blood Flow

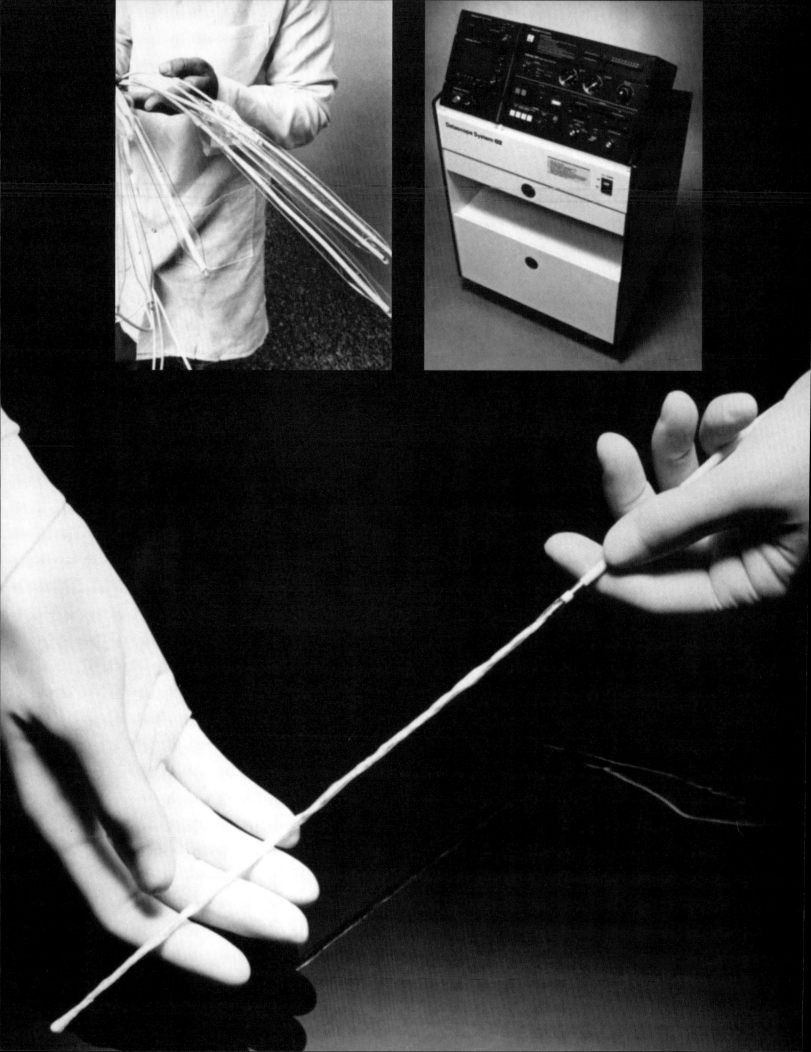

SALES AND SERVICE

In 1972, only one year after Datascope opened Datascope B.V., its overseas subsidiary in Holland, international sales already represented about 17 percent of the company's total sales.[33] That summer, the company formed a Domestic International Sales Corporation (DISC) that would further promote sales of its products overseas while receiving tax benefits from new federal legislation designed to encourage exports.[34] And in 1978, the company opened Datascope GmbH, a subsidiary in Düsseldorf, Germany.

Datascope's international business grew steadily, thanks in large part to the devoted direct sales effort of Datascope B.V. In 1975, Datascope B.V. and DISC brought in $1.5 million in sales, followed by $2.4 million in 1976. Also, beginning in 1975 the company began expanding its marketing efforts to the Far East, the Middle East, and South America.[35] The balloon pumps, in particular, sold well in Japan and were sold in countries all over the world — even in such unlikely places as communist Europe, Cuba, and China.[36]

In the latter part of the decade, Datascope's domestic marketing force grew stronger as the company added more direct sales and service staff in areas that contained the majority of the country's hospital beds. Datascope also sold its products through independent distributors, but by then Datascope had decided to gradually eliminate distributors and transition to direct sales in the United States.

One of these important sales and service hires was Warren Shoop, who came on board in 1976 as national service manager and later became vice president of worldwide service. Nearly 25 years later, Shoop recalled the transition as Datascope expanded its sales and service to a national level and moved into direct

sales. "I came to Datascope to put together a national service force," he said. "Prior to my arrival, Datascope had a small service organization that worked out of the factory and covered a small area in the Northeast. The rest of the United States was covered by dealers and distributors. I came aboard, and Datascope decided to start to go direct with its own sales people."[37]

"We probably had a good 30 distributors in the United States when I came on board in 1977," said Mark Rappaport, director of service operations for Patient Monitoring. "By the early 1980s, there were maybe three or four left."[38]

The buildup of a direct sales force paid off significantly in 1979, when direct sales of all Datascope products rose by 37 percent over the previous fiscal year. As George Heller observed, "Moving to direct sales helped us further grow the business."[39]

Under Warren Shoop's direction, Datascope also started building a reputation for excellent service and support. Each of the company's service representatives was highly knowledgeable about all of Datascope's products and could train service technicians and biomedical engineers to perform maintenance and repair. And, as Shoop pointed out, "As more products came out, we needed to put more people in the field;" it didn't take long to build up a national service staff.[40]

In 1977, Bob Velebir, who had joined Datascope the year before and later became senior tech support instructor and training instructor for Cardiac Assist, moved to Los Angeles to

Opposite: In 1979, Datascope introduced Percor, the world's first percutaneous intra-aortic balloon catheter. Percor revolutionized the field of balloon pumping because it eliminated the need for arterial surgery to insert it.

Right: Datascope attended trade shows all over the world. Its products sold particularly well in Japan, where this 1975 photo was taken.

THE HISTORY OF MEDICAL DEVICE REGULATION

UNTIL THE 1930S, ANY FORM OF MEDI-cal device, whether it was effective or not, could be sold directly to the public. The Postal Fraud Statutes of 1872 prevented interstate shipment of undesirable food and drugs, and the Food and Drug Act of 1906 federally regulated food and drugs. But it wasn't until the Food, Drug and Cosmetic Act of 1938 that the government exerted authority over adulterated and misbranded medical devices. The newly created Food and Drug Administration (FDA) regulated cosmetics and medical devices in addition to food and drugs, but the regulation of medical devices was limited to seizing adulterated or misbranded products only after they reached the market.

Already hard pressed to keep up with the many fraudulent devices being introduced, the FDA became even more strained after World War II, when a revolution in biomedical technology resulted in a torrent of new medical devices. The Drug Amendments of 1962 required the FDA to give premarket approval before new drugs could be marketed, but the constraint didn't apply to new medical devices. Premarket approval for medical devices was not required until the Medical Device Amendments of 1976, when the FDA ranked all medical devices into a three-tiered classification based on their risk and imposed premarketing procedures to regulate each category. The 1976 amendments also dealt with good manufacturing practices and gave the FDA authority to ban dangerous products and order manufacturers to recall, repair, or refund defective devices.

Fourteen years later, the Safe Medical Devices Act of 1990 regulated the safety and effectiveness of devices and strengthened the FDA's authority to monitor marketed products, which made the premarket review faster and less rigid. The Medical Device Amendments of 1992 broadened medical device reporting and postmarket surveillance and boosted FDA power to require repairs, replacements, and refunds.[1]

open Datascope's first regional office. "I was basically staying out there to very nonchalantly set up West Coast operations for service," he said. "I had a picture of the office, and I brought it to George Heller one day. He went running into Larry's office, saying, 'Larry, look! There's a building out in Los Angeles with the name Datascope on it!' They were thrilled about that."[41]

UPKEEP

While Datascope was growing its product lines and increasing its research and development efforts, it also began making key appointments to its executive staff. In 1974, Saper hired Paul Arnstein as director of manufacturing; Richard Laskey as vice president for biochemical research; William Terrell as director of corporate design; and John Zlock as chief of mechanical design. These new officers joined Datascope's seasoned ranks, which included Larry Saper as president and treasurer; George Heller as vice president for sales and corporate secretary; Ernst Janzen as managing director of Datascope B.V., and Matt Mahoney as product planning specialist.[42] The following year saw more appointments: Harmon Aronson joined as director of engineering; Bruce Hanson, a mechanical engineer, came on board to manage IABP manufacturing and head up IABP research and development; and David Hitchcoff became sales manager. Another important hire came in 1976 when Amnon Goldstein, a former director of engineering at technology giant Litton Industries, joined the company as vice president of engineering. And in 1978, Stuart Levy came on board as controller and assistant treasurer.

In fiscal year 1973, the same year it moved its headquarters and production facilities to Paramus, New Jersey, Datascope realized $3.1 million in sales, an amazing increase over the previous year.[43] Sales continued to skyrocket, nearing $10 million in 1976. Earnings crossed the $1 million threshold in 1976, reaching $1.3 million. And all of this sustained growth had been achieved without acquiring other companies and while keeping virtually free of short- and long-term debt.

By 1976, Datascope's manufacturing operations had outgrown the facility in Paramus, and the company bought a 40,000-square-foot building in Oakland, New Jersey, for research, development, and manufacture of Datascope's disposable products, which included the intra-aortic balloon and the PAD.[44]

Since he founded Datascope in 1964, Larry Saper had been intimately involved in the company's business. In 1975, Saper didn't stop living and breathing Datascope, but he did

Above and below: In 1976, Larry Saper married Carol Schops. Their first child, Adam, was born a year later on Saper's birthday — just as Carol had planned.

make room for the love of his life when he married Carol Schops. Their first child, Adam, was born a year later, on September 8, Larry's birthday. Another son, Alex, was born on April 22, 1983.

THE GOVERNMENT STEPS IN

For many years, U.S. manufacturers of medical devices had free rein to create products that met a need in any area of medicine, and the government did not intervene. But for the safety of the general public and the medical industry at large, in 1976, the federal government began regulating such products under the guidelines set forth by the Food and Drug Administration (FDA).

The Medical Device Amendments bill was introduced by Senator Ted Kennedy and signed into law in May 1976. The law regulated manufacturing practices and established standards for producing medical devices. It also required new products to be approved by the FDA before they could be marketed. Though the law was necessary to protect Americans from fraudulent or harmful devices, complying with it required significantly more administrative work and expense.[45]

"The medical device law was no big surprise, but I wouldn't say we were prepared for it," Saper said more than two decades later. "We created a responsibility for submissions and added infrastructure to exercise that responsibility."[46]

Gary Mohr, Datascope's regulatory and patent attorney, explained how getting approval from the FDA could sometimes be a waiting game. "It's a frustrating process for any company because you want to market your product the same day it's ready to go out," he said. "But you can't do that. You have to submit data to the FDA and then wait to sell."[47]

Mohr explained how companies might be able to speed up the regulatory process.

In your submission, the more data you can give the better, and you can show that it's similar to another product, even though it might work better, but that's the most proactive you can be. If it's a PMA [pre-market approval] where you don't have a similar product already on the market [categorized as Class III], then you have to do a lot of clinical work to show that it's useful and safe. You can go to the FDA and speak to people if there's a problem as opposed to writing a letter, but you can't advertise, and there's no assistance you can give them other than giving them good data and being able to explain the product in a clear manner.[48]

Still, Mohr said, getting the FDA to grant permission to market a unique, Class III product could take from six months to two years, "depending on how much data they need, how clear it is that the product's safe, and how clear it is that it's useful and effective."[49]

Such regulation might have been a stumbling block for a young company like Datascope, but Larry Saper had long been devoted to creating products that adhered to the highest standards. As Saper noted in his 1976 letter to shareholders, "We believe that we will be able to comply with applicable regulations when adopted."[50]

Datascope was, indeed, able to comply. "Sales were rising faster than any expenses the new act caused," Saper said. But he acknowledged that the regulatory process "was something we had to learn, and the learning process took place over some time."[51]

A GOOD PLACE TO BE

Even as the company grew larger and more complex, it managed to retain the entrepreneurial spirit and closely knit culture that began with Larry Saper and George Heller. "As soon as I walked in the door for my interview, I saw that Datascope was a very relaxed company," said Susan Chapman, who began assisting Saper in 1975. "Mr. Saper was in jeans, and I thought, 'Well, I'm going to fit right in here.' It was very comfortable from the minute I walked in the door."[52]

One of Chapman's first tasks after she was hired was to pick up cheese and bread for a company celebration. "That's how we did things," she said. "If a big order came in, we would send somebody out to get ice cream for everyone."[53]

She also noted the sense of camaraderie among employees. "Everyone worked together," she said. "If it meant staying until 10 o'clock at

Heart bene...

Cardiologists: 'Good life' could be short life

Dozens of heart specialists are strung out for blocks as they jog along Collins Avenue this morning

George Heller, sales manager extraordinaire as well as the company's senior vice president and secretary, participated in a Heart Benefit run in Miami, Florida.

Larry Saper playing with his sons, Adam (right) and Alex. Before he created a family with his wife, Carol, Saper had already created a family at Datascope, a place where employees felt relaxed, empowered, and proud to work.

night to get something done, we did it. No one ever had a problem about doing what they had to do to get the product out the door."[54]

Warren Shoop agreed. "We would all help each other out," he said. "If the floor had to be swept, we in the service department might do that. Or we might help out in the test department. It was just a real group effort."[55]

"We knew practically everyone in the company," said Bob Hamilton, who joined Datascope's test department in 1972 and later became principal engineer of the Cardiac Assist division. "And everyone did whatever it took to get a quality product out the door. I'd do my job, which was testing and calibrating systems, but then I'd spend time in the shipping department, boxing up stuff. Everyone took their job very seriously and wanted to do a good job, and that hasn't changed."[56]

"Everyone was hands on," said Mark Rappaport. "Mr. Saper, too, was extremely involved in the day-to-day business and the direction of the company. Innovation and bringing out new products were paramount in our growth, just as it still is today."[57]

Datascope truly cared about the welfare of its employees and was committed to offering them ample opportunities and benefits. In addition, the company cultivated creativity and gave employees latitude to learn and grow.

In 1976, the company adopted a noncontributory pension plan and employee stock ownership plan, and Rappaport remembered the company's health benefits package as being "very elaborate.… Even at a time when larger companies than us started charging for health benefits, Datascope never did. It fully paid for all health benefits, and that didn't have to change until the late 1980s."[58]

Rappaport, who prior to working for Datascope had frequently switched jobs, knew from his first day of work that he had made a good decision in joining the company. His first scheduled work day was July 4, 1976. "But that was a holiday," he said. "I got paid for it, and I didn't have to come in until July 5. I knew by the time I closed the first day that I didn't have to look for the right job anymore."[59]

Fred Adelman, who joined Datascope in 1979 as accounting manager and later became corporate controller, remembered his first impressions of Stuart Levy (his immediate boss), Larry Saper's mission, and Datascope.

I interviewed with Stuart Levy and immediately liked him. He was interesting, young, dynamic. He had a lot of new plans. Then I interviewed with Larry Saper. That was an incredible interview. He was just so knowledgeable and charismatic. I thought, "Wow! This is some company! I would love to work for this company." Datascope was making products that were helpful to society, and that really enticed me too. I saw coming to work here as a great opportunity.[60]

As a result of Datascope's salutary work environment, its employees did not feel a need to form a union, even at a time when most other manufacturers in New Jersey had unions. On three occasions in Datascope's history, in fact, employees voted down attempts to unionize. "That's because Mr. Saper has always been concerned for the employees and recognized that the employees are the key to Datascope's growth and success," said Rappaport. "The company treats employees well, so there's been no need for a third party to intercede."[61]

A REVELATION IN IABP THERAPY

In May 1979, Datascope's cardiac assist business took a giant leap when the company introduced one of its most innovative and important contributions to the medical device industry: Percor, the world's first percutaneous intra-aortic balloon catheter. The FDA gave its approval for the device later in the year, and the product was put on the U.S. market in December 1979.[62]

The significance of this invention was staggering. No longer did the intra-aortic balloon have to be inserted surgically. Rather, the percutaneous balloon catheter could be inserted through the skin by an arterial puncture, which made it appealing to interventional cardiologists. Datascope's IABP technology was now accessible to every medical facility with a cardiac catheterization lab.

"Datascope's first intra-aortic balloon pump was [more] invasive," explained Dr. Joseph Grayzel, "and that was one of the impediments in the field. The cardiologist or even other surgeons would have to call a vascular surgeon to come in and place this device in the femoral artery."[63]

"We invented the ability to wrap up a balloon so that it fit into a sheath," Saper said. "You go through the skin with a needle puncture and puncture the artery. Then you put in a wire and dilator to dilate the path through the arterial wall. And then you introduce the balloon through the sheath dilator. Before, the balloon had to be implanted surgically, which required a cut down through the skin to the artery. A slit was made in the artery, and then a graft was sewn in, and the catheter was put in through the graft."[64]

In addition, the percutaneous balloon catheter entailed far fewer complications than the surgical method.[65] As Grayzel observed, Datascope's percutaneous intra-aortic balloon catheter "changed the whole field" of intra-aortic counterpulsation. An article by the Associated Press published in September 1980 explained just how groundbreaking the new balloon was.

The new device can be implanted by a skilled physician in about five minutes, compared to the 30-minute surgical operation required for the standard intra-aortic balloon pump.... [It] can

even be used during emergency cardio-pulmonary resuscitation, something that was impossible with earlier versions.

The standard procedure has been to have a surgeon open the femoral artery... and attach a surgical sleeve through which the balloon is inserted. From there, guided by a continuous X-ray picture, doctors maneuver the balloon into position in the aorta.

But with the new pump, surgery is unnecessary. A hollow tube is inserted through the skin of the leg into the artery so the pump can be moved through the artery to the heart. The result is fewer complications, since there is no surgery.[66]

GREAT MINDS

The percutaneous intra-aortic balloon catheter was co-invented by two men: Sidney Wolvek, who in 1967 had designed and fabricated the implantable intra-aortic balloon catheters for Adrian Kantrowitz's research, and Bruce Hanson, who in 1979 became Datascope's vice president for operations. Wolvek had joined Datascope in 1975 as director of advanced research in cardiac assist and later became director

Bruce Hanson (left), vice president for operations of disposable products, and Sidney Wolvek (right), director of advanced research in cardiac assist, co-invented the revolutionary percutaneous intra-aortic balloon catheter.

Above left: Dr. David Bregman, who co-invented the dual-chambered intra-aortic balloon, was a vital consultant to Datascope for many years.

Above right: Ernst Janzen, head of international sales, was instrumental in selling Datascope's products abroad.

of scientific research. He played an integral role in Datascope's history, both as a clinical trainer and as an inventor.[67]

"We knew from the start that if we wanted to expand IABP use, we had to make it simpler to insert the balloon," Hanson said. "It's great to say that, but it's another thing to do it."[68]

Hanson and Wolvek began studying ways to make the balloon smaller so that it could be inserted through the skin, yet still large enough to function effectively in the comparatively large human aorta. They experimented for three years before achieving the results they wanted. They invented a process for wrapping the balloon around a stylet, or wire, to shrink its bulk.

Dr. David Bregman and his colleagues at Columbia-Presbyterian Medical Center in New York used the percutaneous balloon catheter on a patient for the first time in early 1979. In the first 27 clinical evaluations, Bregman reported, it saved the lives of 21 patients.[69]

As with the first IABP system and the PAD, clinical acceptance of the percutaneous balloon catheter did not come instantly — but it did come quickly. Saper was optimistic in his 1979 report to shareholders. "Because the percutaneous bal-

loon converts IABP to a non-surgical procedure," he wrote, "we believe that clinical acceptance of this device should result in a substantial increase in Datascope's share of the IABP market in the medical management of cardiac patients." Indeed, by the time the FDA had given its approval to market the device, it had undergone 64 successful clinical evaluations.[70]

As history would soon prove, Datascope's percutaneous intra-aortic balloon catheter was a major breakthrough for the medical profession, and the invention catapulted Datascope into the limelight as a tremendously significant and innovative company.[71]

A SOLID FUTURE

There is no doubt that Datascope achieved an important status as the creator of the percutaneous balloon, but the company's dynamic sales force and clinical education in the field also contributed to its run of success. George Heller now focused most of his sales efforts in the area of cardiac assist in the United States and Japan, and Ernst Janzen made great strides in Europe. International sales in both Europe and the Far East grew vigorously and in 1979 rose to $4.8 million, which accounted for 30 percent of Datascope's total sales.[72]

Training doctors and hospital staff in the use of Datascope's products was another necessary component in the company's success. Both George Heller and Ernst Janzen began conducting international seminars, even in countries behind the iron curtain, such as Czechoslovakia, Hungary, and Poland.[73]

Also in 1979, Datascope established a marketing services department to help it develop a corporate image by designing all its promotional brochures and annual reports. The department also coordinated the collateral material needed for trade shows and sales meetings. Oscar Arnay was hired as the first director of marketing services, and his efforts helped reinforce Datascope's image as a company with great ideas and great products.[74]

Datascope ended fiscal 1979 with $15.9 million in sales, a 16 percent increase over the previous year. But in the years to follow, the percutaneous intra-aortic balloon catheter and more innovations in monitoring would lead to far greater growth.[75]

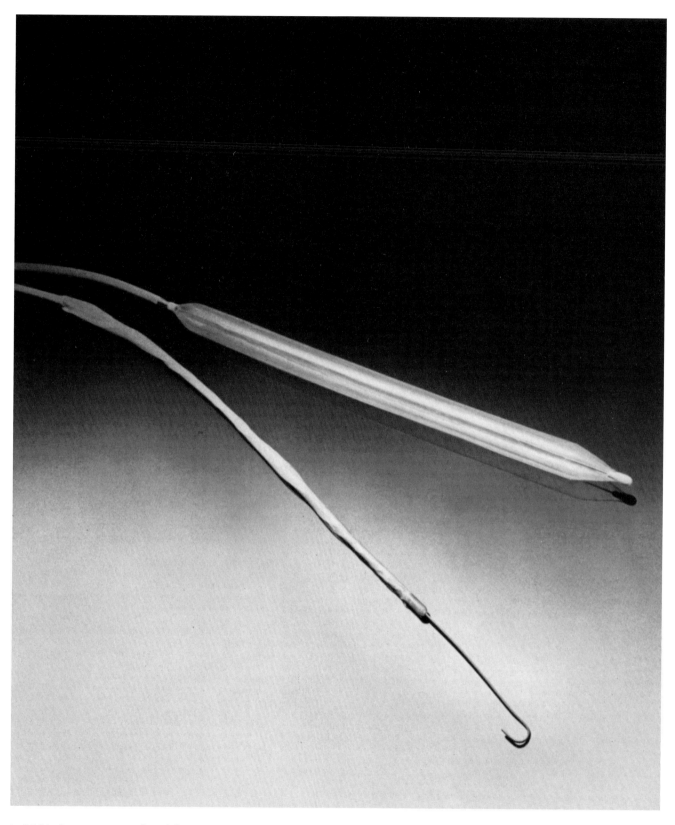

In 1981, Datascope introduced the Percor-DL, a percutaneous intra-aortic balloon with a dual-lumen catheter. A guidewire helped the user direct the catheter to the aorta and was particularly appealing to cardiologists who were accustomed to using guidewires in cardiac catheterizations.

CHAPTER FIVE

MATCHING INNOVATION TO NEED

1980–1985

Innovation is always our goal. But it isn't enough simply to have a commitment to techno-logical excellence. The key to our success begins with the closest possible orientation to the market – to the physician working in the hospital. Our market niches are defined not only by our technology but by our customers.

— Larry Saper, 1985

THE 1980S WAS A DECADE OF unprecedented upheaval and uncertainty in the healthcare industry. As Americans became more knowledgeable about their health, they demanded better healthcare. And as medical costs in the 1980s escalated at an astounding rate, they also wanted more for their money.[1]

Persistence of poor quality and rising costs led to a minor revolution in healthcare during this time. Medical professionals received improved training, healthcare organizations were strengthened, and performance was continually improved. Governmental and healthcare organizations also began reassessing credentials and quality.[2]

Datascope, dedicated to quality healthcare through innovative products, was in a prime position to facilitate the growing trend toward improved healthcare. And as the country's medical needs grew, Datascope continued to match innovation to need and realized exceptional success in the process.

PLANNING FOR THE LONG TERM

Throughout the 1980s, Datascope continually invested in long-term growth through research and development (R&D) of new products and through expanding its direct sales, service, and marketing resources. In the late 1970s, Datascope had begun transitioning from a distributor-based network to

direct sales and service, and by the early 1980s the transition was complete. The company went from 49 direct sales and service people in 1980 to 131 worldwide representatives in 1985.

Taking some of the burden off sales representatives, in 1981, Datascope started the first accredited clinical education program in the field to provide training to physicians, nurses, and technicians on its IABP system. The clinical education program was the brainchild of Donna Goebel, a registered nurse who joined Datascope after working with the balloon pump in the cardiac intensive care unit of the Cleveland Clinic. Registered nurses with experience in managing patients were ideal for teaching the intricacies of balloon pumping.

By 1985, the clinical education services department, directed by Marjorie Self, consisted of two regional managers and seven other experts in IABP therapy – all with advanced training in critical care nursing. The team held training seminars and conducted in-service classes at hospitals throughout the United States and Europe. The team

The Datatrac was a tremendous aid to the anesthesiologist because it automatically printed a complete record and trend of all monitored data on the anesthesia record chart, thus eliminating the burden of record keeping.

also provided 24-hour troubleshooting to hospitals that needed direction or advice.[3]

"Our clinical field support staff has been outstanding," said Dr. Joseph Grayzel. "They're not selling, but supporting the customers. These are people who go to hospitals while cases are being done. They work with people, show them how to optimize the operation of the system, make sure that the timing they're setting [on the balloon pump] is the best timing for the particular patient, explain to them the physiology of balloon pumping."[4]

Datascope also stepped up its service efforts by developing a technical support department (initially made up of three people) to train biomedical engineers, hospital personnel, distributors, and service representatives in the technical aspects of Datascope's products. The department also held regional technical service seminars.

Years later, Marty Nussbaum, Datascope's outside general counsel, attributed the company's clinical education and service to its leading market position. "It's not only the quality of the

Datascope began its formal clinical education services department in 1981. The department was staffed by registered nurses who were experts in critical care.

product," he said, "but also the service relationship that Datascope builds with the customers and the clinical education and assistance it offers to professionals."[5]

Many new executives joined the company or were promoted from within during this time. These included Jeffrey Arnold as vice president of operations, Andre Cohen as vice president of international marketing, Gregory Buis as vice president of marketing, and Ralph Lyng as vice president of an upstart division, implantable devices. Promotions included William Terrell as vice president of corporate design, Ernst Janzen as senior vice president of international, and George Heller as senior vice president and secretary.

At the same time, Datascope was adding to its physical facilities. In 1980, the company opened a 22,000-square-foot instrumentation manufacturing facility across from its Paramus headquarters and expanded the Oakland plant to increase balloon catheter production.[6]

Datascope's continued investment in R&D, sales and service, and operations paid off handsomely for the company – and for investors. For fiscal 1980, Datascope's sales increased 30 percent over the previous year to $20.7 million, and earnings swelled 77 percent to $1.3 million. The following year saw even more growth as sales grew 51 percent to $31.2 million and earnings increased an amazing 103 percent to $2.7 million.

More importantly, however, Datascope's dedication to service and R&D had paid off for customers: the hospitals that used Datascope products and the patients who benefited from them.

EXTENUATING CIRCUMSTANCES

In the early 1980s, the United States was slowly pulling out of an economic recession, even while the healthcare industry was in the midst of a crisis and poised on the brink of major change. The most profound change came in 1983, when Congress passed sweeping amendments to Medicare in a drastic effort to control spiraling healthcare costs and protect Medicare from bankruptcy. Reflecting Congress's concern over rapidly rising medical costs, the bill made one of recent history's fastest trips through the House and Senate.[7]

The new amendments brought about the most significant changes in Medicare's 18-year existence by changing the way the nation's acute care hospitals billed Medicare for services. The

Above: Larry Saper at Datascope's Holland facility in 1985.

Right: The M/D3A monitor-defibrillator system was perfectly suited for the busy operating room.

direct sales force helped pick up the slack. Overall sales for fiscal 1984 grew 12 percent to $42.2 million, and sales for 1985 increased 19.7 percent to $50.6 million.

NEW DEFIBRILLATOR SYSTEMS

Shortly after the release of the highly successful M/D3 defibrillator system, Datascope introduced a companion SM3 support module that allowed the M/D3 to be used on an emergency cart without sacrificing its portability. The SM3 support module made the M/D3 more flexible and turned it into a hospital system. It contained a built-in defibrillator energy tester and allowed recharging of the M/D3's batteries. It also allowed the M/D3 to be operated from the power line.[9]

As testament to the M/D3's quality, in 1980 the U.S. Air Force chose it to use on board its aeromedical evacuation aircraft. The M/D3 was also chosen for use at the 1980 Olympic Winter Games.[10]

As healthcare prices escalated in the early 1980s and as the U.S. economy struggled out of the doldrums, Datascope saw more price competition, especially among defibrillators. To

law dictated that Medicare reimbursements would be driven by diagnostic-related groups (DRGs), which formed the bedrock of the law's Prospective Payment System (PPS). Under the PPS, hospitals no longer could charge Medicare according to their costs. Instead, they would be reimbursed only a predetermined amount for a diagnosed illness. Any treatment expenses incurred over this set Medicare amount would have to be absorbed by the hospital.[8]

Meanwhile, the economy was taking its toll on international sales as a strong U.S. dollar lowered demand for Datascope's products and increased local competition. In 1983, the company opened another international subsidiary, this one in the United Kingdom. Weak European sales, especially in Holland, which had historically been a strong market for Datascope, were offset by strong sales in the United Kingdom and Germany.

Datascope's sales slowed in 1983 as a direct result of the new Medicare DRG reimbursement system, which caused hospitals to tighten their belts and cut costs, and the weak international market. But the company's talented and tenacious

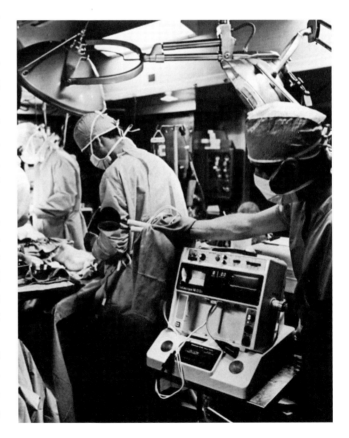

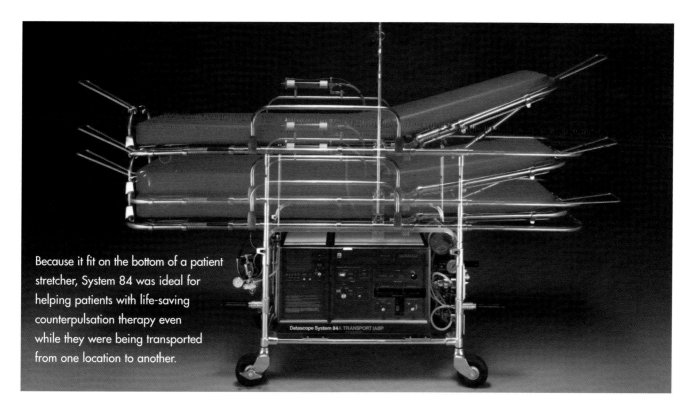

Because it fit on the bottom of a patient stretcher, System 84 was ideal for helping patients with life-saving counterpulsation therapy even while they were being transported from one location to another.

help offset rising inflation, Datascope introduced the M/D3A defibrillator system in 1981, which was less expensive to produce than its predecessor. Moreover, it had two new controls for setting automatic high and low heart rate alarms, which alerted emergency room staff to life-threatening changes in the patient's heart rhythm.[11] In 1985, Datascope released the M/D4, a lower-priced alternative to the M/D3A that offered a separable monitor.[12]

The M/D3A and M/D4 were well accepted, but increased competition, especially from the Physio-Control unit of Eli Lilly & Company, prohibited Datascope's defibrillator sales from keeping pace with escalating sales of its other product lines. In 1986, the company stopped manufacturing them. "I felt we were no longer competitive," Saper said. "We didn't have the resources to compete, and I couldn't see an easy path to get the resources – not with all of our other product lines."[13]

IABP DEVELOPMENTS

Clinical response to the revolutionary Percor (which Datascope patented in 1980), the first IABP catheter capable of being inserted without surgery, grew steadily since Datascope introduced it in late 1979. As Dr. Joseph Grayzel observed, "The

percutaneous balloon absolutely broke open the IABP market, and the field, over the next 10 years, continued to expand."[14]

The Percor's unique, groundbreaking benefits created strong and rapid growth in the IABP market and made Datascope the leader in IABP therapy. From 1979 to 1982, Datascope's IABP sales tripled while competitors scrambled to come up with their own niches or committed patent infringements on Datascope's Percor. By the summer of 1982, Percor was being used regularly in nearly all the hospitals with Datascope balloon pumps and the majority of hospitals that used competitors' balloon pumps. IABP therapy was also being used more frequently because Percor was so much faster and simpler to use than previous intra-aortic balloon catheters.[15]

The Percor greatly simplified intra-aortic balloon pumping, and that meant the life-saving therapy could be used in the thousands of community hospitals where the majority of cardiac patients are first brought – hospitals that did not have open-heart surgery capabilities. Datascope's clinical services professionals helped encourage wider use of IABP, especially in community hospitals, by educating clinicians about the therapy's benefits and ease of use.

More innovations in intra-aortic balloon pumping soon followed. Datascope's System 84 transport pump, which debuted in 1981, fit an intra-aortic balloon pump on a cart connected to the bottom of a patient stretcher. Like the Percor, the System 84 helped promote IABP therapy in community hospitals because it allowed IABP to be performed while transporting a patient to open-heart hospitals.[16]

The Percor's success led to increased sales of the System 82 as well as new developments in intra-aortic balloon catheters. In 1981, Datascope introduced the Percor-DL, a dual-lumen version of the original Percor. The first lumen was used for inflation and deflation, and the second lumen contained a guidewire to help thread the balloon catheter into the aorta. Once in position, the second lumen could be used to provide a blood path to measure central arterial pressure and sample arterial blood.[17] The Percor-DL II, released in 1982, was an improved dual-lumen catheter, and the Percor 10.5 Fr., also released in 1982, was a single-lumen device that took up 22 percent less space in the aorta.[18]

The Percor 10.5 Fr. used a balloon catheter that had a diameter of 10.5 Fr. (1 Fr. = $\frac{1}{3}$ mm). The smaller the diameter of the catheter, the easier it is to insert and the less interference with normal blood flow in the artery; thus, the Percor 10.5 Fr.'s smaller size was a significant improvement over the original Percor, which measured 12 Fr.

In addition, the Percor 10.5 Fr. used helium rather than carbon dioxide to inflate the balloon. Helium, because of its lower molecular weight, could inflate and deflate the balloon more quickly through a smaller tube, which allowed Datascope to eventually refine the pneumatic subsystem of the IABP to create certain advantages. Jonathan Williams, who joined Datascope in 1985 and later became a director of engineering in the Cardiac Assist division, explained.

As we've refined the pneumatic subsystem of the pump, which is responsible for determin-

ing how fast the balloon deflates, we've been able to reduce the diameter of the tube that goes between the balloon and the outside world. That means the indwelling portion of the catheter that's going to the patient can be smaller, and there are two chief benefits to this. First, the size of the perforation to introduce the catheter can be smaller, so potential bleeding at the site after the procedure can be managed better. Second, because the catheter occupies less cross-sectional area, the residual area that's available for blood flow around it can be larger.[19]

Also in 1982, Datascope released System 83, the next-generation balloon pump. Not only was System 83 easier to operate than its predecessor; it also featured a pacemaker rejection circuit (to prevent implantable pacemakers from interfering with balloon pumping) and a pressure display module so the benefits of IABP therapy could be measured. In addition, System 83 could pump either carbon dioxide or helium, which made it suitable for any of Datascope's balloon catheters.[20] The System 84A transport pump came out the following year and incorporated the technical advances of the System 83.

Just as Datascope had intended, the transport pump helped move intra-aortic balloon pumping into community hospitals. A story in the *Daily Journal*, of Union County, New Jersey, told how a balloon pump at Elizabeth General Medical Center saved Dorothy Vargas's life after she suffered her second heart attack. "Advances that have made the equipment transportable now enable community hospitals that do not perform heart surgery to use the pump to save

Datascope's percutaneous intra-aortic balloon catheters came in several different sizes to suit the needs of the patient. Over the years, Datascope would be a leader in creating balloon catheters with increasingly smaller diameters.

a patient's life before he or she can be moved to another facility," the article concluded.[21]

The trend toward smaller balloon catheters continued, and in 1983, Datascope introduced the dual-lumen Percor-DL 10.5 Fr. to replace the Percor-DL II. That same year, the company began marketing the Percor 9.5 Fr. (which took up 20 percent less area in the aorta than the Percor 10.5 Fr.) and the Percor 8.5 Fr. (which took up 42 percent less area than the Percor 10.5). At the time, the 8.5 Fr. was the smallest balloon catheter on the market.[22]

Frank Frisch, senior manufacturing manager for the Cardiac Assist division, explained why smaller is better.

We're always trying to make them smaller and smaller so the size of the hole that's put into the femoral artery is smaller and you get less bleeding. Also, a smaller catheter takes up less space in the patient's femoral artery, increasing the blood flow around the catheter to the leg.[23]

Frisch also explained the challenges Datascope faced when trying to make the balloon catheters smaller.

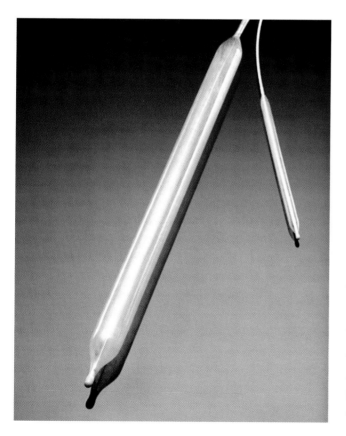

Years ago, the technology of the pump did not allow it to shuttle the helium in and out of the balloon fast enough with a smaller catheter. Also, we were taking up a lot of volume in the catheter with the inner lumen, which is a smaller tube inside a catheter tubing that serves as the shuttle passage for the helium. The inner lumen supports a guidewire, which is used to insert the balloon into the aorta, and if you start taking up too much volume with that inner lumen, you reduce the diameter of the shuttle passage.[24]

SAVING INFANTS' LIVES

Datascope's IABP innovations kept coming. In 1984, Datascope introduced the first balloon catheter made specifically to help infants. To develop it, Datascope worked with St. Christopher's Hospital for Children, in Philadelphia, loaning an IABP system free of charge to aid in the research. The standard balloon had to be completely redesigned for a much smaller heart and arteries, and that presented unique challenges. Adult balloons were inflated with about 40 cc of air, but balloons for infants up to six months old had be much smaller – only 2.5 cc of air was needed to inflate them. For children up to age seven, the balloon was inflated with 7.5 cc of air.[25]

Sales of the pediatric balloon catheters were small, and it was not financially profitable for Datascope to manufacture them, but they filled a desperate need that no other company had filled and underscored Datascope's commitment to saving lives.[26]

"It takes more time to build a pediatric catheter in comparison to building an adult catheter," explained Frisch. "You're talking about three to three-and-a-half hours to build each one."[27]

But Datascope didn't manufacture the pediatric balloon catheters for financial reward, observed Frisch. Rather, the reward came with the knowledge that Datascope was saving

Datascope created the first intra-aortic balloon catheter for infants. Whereas adult balloon catheters were inflated with about 40 cc of helium, the pediatric balloon catheter was inflated with only 2.5 cc. The tremendous size difference (shown at left) made the pediatric balloon catheter extremely complicated to design and expensive to manufacture.

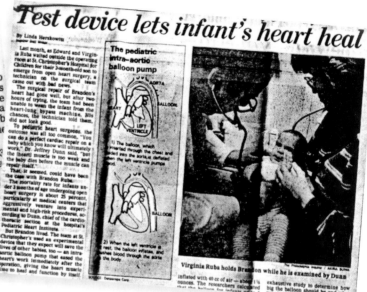

Pump Helps Infants' Hearts

PHILADELPHIA, Feb. 9 (UPI) — A balloon pump designed to ease strain on the heart after cardiac surgery has been modified to work in infants, a doctor says.

The device, used in adults since the early 1970's, has become available for infants in the last six months, Dr. Jeffrey Dunn, chief of the cardiothoracic section of St. Christopher's Hospital for Children, said Wednesday.

Dr. Dunn said the balloon pump, by providing the heart with a resting period while it recovers, improves newborns' chances of surviving cardiac surgery.

A polyurethylene balloon is surgically placed in the aorta, the body's main artery, and is attached by a thin tube to a pump outside the body. The balloon's job is to help the left ventricle.

After the ventricle pushes blood into the aorta, the balloon inflates and helps push the blood through the body. The balloon then deflates, making a vacuum to ease the ventricle's job when it again pushes blood into the aorta.

A sick infant's heart rate is from 1? to 200 beats a minute, but an adult ba loon pump operates at 120 beats minute, Dr. Dunn said. It took searchers at St. Christopher's m than three years to perfect a syst fast enough for infants, and sn enough to fit into an infant's aorti

When an infant's heart is st enough to beat on its own, the ballc removed.

Test device lets infant's heart heal

By Linda Herskowitz

Last month, as Edward and Virgin ia Ruba waited outside the operating room at St. Christopher's Hospital for Children for their 2-month-old son to emerge from open heart surgery, a technician on the surgical team came out with bad news.

The surgical repair of Brandon's heart had gone well, but after two hours of trying, the team was unable to wean the infant from the heart-lung bypass machine. His chances, the technician told them, did not look good.

To pediatric heart surgeons, the outcome was all too common. "You can do a perfect cardiac repair on a baby which you know will ultimately work," Dr. Jeffrey Dunn said, "but the [heart] muscle is too weak and the baby dies before the muscle can repair itself."

That, it seemed, could have been the case with Brandon Ruba.

The mortality rate for infants under 3 months of age undergoing open heart surgery is about 25 percent, particularly at medical centers that aggressively venture into experimental and high-risk procedures, according to Dunn, chief of the cardiothoracic section at the hospital's Pediatric Heart Institute.

But Brandon lived. The team at St. Christopher's used an experimental device that they expect will save the lives of other babies, too — an intra-aortic balloon pump that eased the heart's work immediately after the operation, giving the heart muscle time to heal and function by itself.

The pediatric intra-aortic balloon pump

1) The balloon, which inserted through the chest and ded into the aorta is deflated the left ventricle pumps od.

2) When the left ventricle is rest, the balloon inflates, and pushes blood through the aorta the body.

Virginia Ruba holds Brandon while he is examined by Dunn

inflated with 40 cc of air — about 1½ ounces. The researchers calculated that the balloon for infants should be exhaustive study to determine how big the balloon should be and what its shape should be." Dr. Jerome

---

Datascope's pediatric balloon catheters made dramatic headlines, and more than a few parents and physicians were grateful for the company's willingness to produce the devices, despite the fact that Datascope didn't profit from doing so.

---

infants' lives. "We've gotten letters from family members who are grateful to Datascope for supplying the balloon that saved their child," Frisch said.[28]

Even with a smaller balloon catheter, intra-aortic balloon pumping for infants involved several difficulties. An infant's aorta is less elastic than an adult's, making it more difficult to safely guide the catheter.[29] Also, a healthy newborn's heart beats from 130 times a minute, and a sick infant's heart beats much faster – from 190 to 200 beats per minute. By contrast, the standard intra-aortic balloon pump, designed for adults, operated at only 120 beats per minute. Datascope worked with St. Christopher's so that the balloon would inflate on alternate beats when the heart was beating faster than about 165 beats a minute.[30]

Dr. Jeffrey Dunn, professor of surgery at St. Christopher's, was particularly grateful for Datascope's pediatric balloon catheters. Only one year after their introduction, he had already used them to save two infants' lives and expected the hospital to be able to save more infants' lives each year.

Every year several thousand children were born in the United States with operable heart defects, and many of these children could not be saved without IABP technology. "One of our frequent dilemmas in pediatric cardiac surgery is that we will need a device that is not financially rewarding for a company to go out and make for us," Dunn said. "Despite the limited commercial value of the pediatric catheter, [Datascope has] been helping us and supporting us. I think that's superb."[31]

One of Dunn's patients was two-month-old Brandon Ruba, who had very little chance of survival after undergoing open-heart surgery at St. Christopher's Hospital because he couldn't be weaned from the heart-lung machine. Unfortunately, many infants younger than three months died after open-heart surgery – 25 percent according to Dunn. But Brandon Ruba survived, thanks to the pediatric balloon catheter and the alterations made to the balloon pump.[32]

As of 2003, Datascope remained the only company to manufacture pediatric balloon catheters.

A LEADER IN MONITORS

As the standards for healthcare continued to rise, Datascope introduced several new physiological monitors in the first half of the decade, all of them engineered for ease of operation. "Datascope has always taken the approach of making our products user-friendly," said Mark Rappaport, director of service operations for the Patient Monitoring division. "We're a very strong engineering-driven, technical company, but we know the users have to learn many new products. Their goal is to manage the patient, and they shouldn't have to be worrying about how to *use* the product that's monitoring the patient."[33]

In 1981, Datascope kicked off an innovative series of automatic noninvasive blood pressure (NIBP) monitors with the Accutorr 1. The Accutorr 1 used a blood pressure cuff that automatically inflated and deflated around the arm at predetermined intervals to read blood pressure.

NIBP monitors were gaining clinical acceptance because they provided better patient care when frequent, but not continuous, blood pressure readings were needed. Bob Terranova, director of engineering for the Patient Monitoring division, explained the advantages and disadvantages of noninvasive blood pressure monitoring versus invasive monitoring. "Measuring blood pressure invasively involves inserting a needle into the brachial artery in the wrist, and the blood pressure is measured directly," he said. "It's more accurate than a cuff around the arm, but it's painful to the patient and far more restrictive."[34]

Not only was the Accutorr 1 more compact than other NIBP monitors, which made it convenient to transport from patient to patient, but it was also faster. On average, it took the Accutorr only 25 seconds to measure and display a patient's heart rate and systolic, diastolic, and average blood pressures. A built-in printer printed the values with date and time. Moreover, the Accutorr 1 could do something other NIBP monitors couldn't: it could print a graph to verify the validity of the measurements and a graph that showed the blood pressure and heart rate trends.[35]

Sales of the Accutorr 1 were robust. In the second full fiscal quarter after its introduction, Datascope received about $1 million in Accutorr orders.[36]

The following year, Datascope enhanced its leading position in providing monitors for the anesthesiologist with the introduction of the 2000 monitor series. In a nod toward Datascope's first product, the Carditron (which was also marketed for the anesthesiologist), the 2000 monitor series quickly became Datascope's flagship monitor product line. Like the Carditron, the 2000 monitor was extremely compact and displayed more information than many larger monitors. It could display ECG and two pressure readings at the same time and digital values from two temperature probes.

The Accutorr monitor line originated in 1981 and was created in response to a growing need for noninvasive blood pressure monitoring.

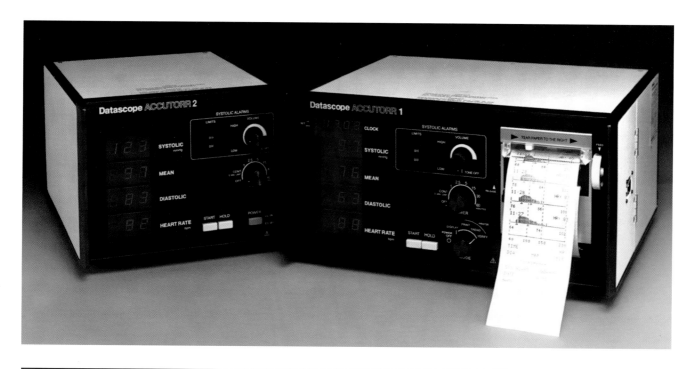

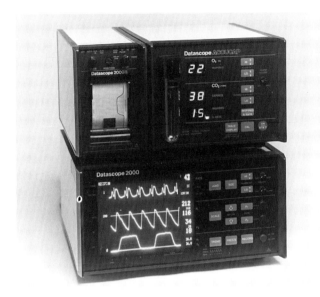

It even displayed a four-hour trend for all the data being monitored. In addition, it eliminated false heart rate readings in patients with pacemakers and prevented electro-surgical interference with the displays. The 2000 monitor could be integrated with the Accutorr in a system so that it displayed the readings of the Accutorr as well.[37]

With the advent of the Accutorr and 2000 monitor series, physiological monitors became the company's fastest-growing product line – yet Datascope had more to offer. In 1983, the Accucap became the next innovation for monitoring patients in the operating room under anesthesia. Accucap was noninvasive and continually monitored how much carbon dioxide the patient was exhaling. Such monitoring gave the anesthesiologist greater control over the patient's respiration and could be an early indicator of problems during anesthesia. The Accucap was also useful for monitoring patients whose breathing was being controlled by a machine. Moreover, the Accucap was easier to use and more accurate than competitive monitors. It was compatible with the Accutorr and 2000 series but could also be used by itself, with a Datascope recorder, or with both the 2000 series and Accutorr.[38]

In 1984, Datascope continued to increase its market share of monitors with several new models aimed primarily at hospitals with fewer than 300 beds. (Such hospitals accounted for about 80 percent of all hospitals).[39] The 2100 monitor integrated ECG, noninvasive blood pressure, and temperature monitoring into one compact package and was ideal for operating rooms, recovery rooms, emergency rooms, and intensive care units. It included a recorder and could print out

Above left: Datascope's System 2000 monitor line represented a new generation of microprocessor-based monitors that displayed more information than larger monitors.

Above right: Developed in 1983, the Accucap CO_2/O_2 monitor provided a noninvasive, continuous measurement of expired carbon dioxide, inhaled oxygen, and respiration rate.

the patient's ECG reading and a 24-hour trend of all monitored data. In addition, the 2100 monitor series was a less-expensive alternative for patients who did not need the invasive pressure monitoring capability of the 2000 monitor.[40]

The Accutorr Central system, another new model, could monitor up to four patients from a remote location by telemetry to bedside monitors and was the first system devoted only to noninvasive blood pressure monitoring. Readings for the four patients were displayed simultaneously on a central monitor, and it could print out the last 72 blood pressure measurements on each patient.[41]

Likewise, the Cenflex central monitor, used mainly in intensive care or critical care units, could display the ECG readings and digital data of up to four patients from a remote location. The system could be expanded to eight patients with the Cenflex +4 Console. The Cenflex Profile, another Datascope innovation, displayed up to four traces, digital data, and eight-hour trend data from any of the eight patients.[42]

Both the Cenflex and the Accutorr Central operated as a system with 2000 series and Accutorr monitors. And because the Cenflex and Accutorr Central increased nursing efficiency, the new monitors helped hospitals address the cost concerns brought on by the new Medicare DRG reimbursement system.[43]

The following year, 1985, Datascope introduced its next innovation: the Accucom heart monitor. This was a revolutionary monitor, for it provided a continuous reading of cardiac output for surgical patients during anesthesia that was much less invasive than the standard method. Measuring cardiac output (the amount of blood the heart beats per minute) was the best way to monitor cardiac performance because a physician could detect, diagnose, and treat serious surgical complications earlier by observing a change in cardiac output, thus reducing the risk of surgery.[44]

Prior to Accucom, physicians had to measure cardiac output by thermodilution, a highly invasive procedure that involved passing a catheter into the pulmonary artery. The method involved serious risks and was expensive, so it was

used only on anesthetized patients who were most likely to development cardiac complications. Accucom was a much safer and less-invasive way to measure cardiac output because it used a specially developed ultrasound probe that was inserted into the esophagus. Thus, Accucom had the potential to make surgery safer for millions of patients who would not otherwise have their cardiac output measured.[45]

"What the Accucom will do, in my view," said Saper, "is to bring the benefit of cardiac output measurement to a great many patients whose condition is not critical enough to warrant the risk and cost of thermodilution. In time, we expect the Accucom to gain acceptance for routine clinical use in anesthesia."[46]

The Accutorr 1 and Datascope 2000 were both revolutionary monitors, and Datascope subsequently introduced other monitors in the same lines.

Or, as George Heller told *Investor's Daily,* "Medicine is evolutionary, not revolutionary, so it will take time [before the new monitor is generally accepted]."[47]

Datatrac, another new monitor, was the first monitor to give the anesthesiologist an automated record of all monitored data. As physicians began monitoring more and more data in the operating room, their record-keeping became more cumbersome. The Datatrac helped lift that burden by automatically printing a record and trend of all monitored data on the anesthesia record chart. Moreover, the Datatrac's unique design allowed the physician to still enter hand-written notes if preferred.[48]

BUILDING A REPUTATION

While Datascope continued pioneering new medical devices and treatments, its status among medical device companies escalated. Corporate Controller Fred Adelman, who joined Datascope in 1979, remembered how Larry Saper's dedication to quality and innovation permeated the company and helped create a reputation for Datascope.

I remember visiting my father-in-law, who was a surgeon in a community hospital, and when he introduced me around, he said, "This is my son-in-law. He works for Datascope." Everybody in the community hospital knew and respected Datascope. That happened other times too. All these people, as soon as they heard the name Datascope, they'd always talk about what a good company it was.[49]

Carol Agnese, who joined Datascope in 1985 and worked her way through several executive administrative positions, attributed the company's excellent reputation to the Datascope people. "Over the years, I've come to realize that it's the people who have made this company. Mr. Saper is a wonderful CEO; he's just a wonderful person to all the employees. And I'm always struck by how nice the people are here. Out in the

Employees and analysts alike praised Larry Saper's genius, dedication, and extraordinary leadership.

field, they give extra service and support because they care about the product and they care about the people the product is serving."[50]

Wall Street was taking notice as well. Shortly after the Accucom was introduced, Datascope was profiled in *Crain's New York Business* under the headline "Profit Gains Provide the Beat at Datascope." The article discussed the company's amazing growth and included comments from Robert Dunne, an analyst at Martin Simpson & Company in Manhattan. "They have been able to keep a product line growing where most people think it has matured," he said. "Datascope's ability to innovate, to see new needs of its customers," had kept the company strong.[51]

Datascope's senior leadership in 1989 included (from left) Joseph Grayzel, Richard Piazza, André Cohen, Murray Pitkowsky, Larry Saper, George Heller, Bruce Hanson, and William Terrell.

CHAPTER SIX

BREAKING NEW GROUND

1986–1990

We have to take care of and stay close to our customers. And taking care of them means understanding what they need and making the best product and, ideally, being there first.

– Larry Saper, 1988

PRESIDENT RONALD REAGAN had effected a tremendous change in Americans' political and economic lives. With the 1981 Economic Recovery Tax Act, he had unveiled an economic policy, later dubbed "Reaganomics," designed to stimulate spending and growth by removing barriers to the flow of money. The new policy lifted oil price controls, cut personal income taxes, and lowered interest rates to stimulate borrowing.

Americans suddenly found themselves with more money and a new sense of confidence. Yet an inherent danger lurked in the rising bubble of American consumerism. Credit was too easy to obtain, and foreign competition had grown stronger. America was running up record debt, both privately and publicly, and newspapers regularly reported on ballooning trade deficits.

Finally, on October 19, 1987, the bubble burst. In a single day, later known as "Black Monday," the Dow Jones industrial average lost 22.6 percent of its value. The stunning drop was a result of the nation's "spiraling indebtedness and chronically high trade deficits," according to one account.

The stock market crash devastated many companies financially, yet Datascope continued its growth pattern, thanks to conservative financing, strong marketing, excellent management, and innovative products. "Our stock price was cut in half by the October crash, then proceeded to make new highs," Saper noted. "It has outperformed the market.... If there is such a

thing as a recession-proof or recession-resistant company, I think we're it."[1]

Once again, Datascope's dedication to long-term research and development (R&D) was paying off. While the company continued to develop innovative products in its existing lines, it was also pioneering in entirely new areas. As Saper observed, "We see the lifeblood of the business in the introduction of new products that are carefully crafted to meet the customers' needs."[2]

Over and over, Datascope was able to recognize a technology's potential and, through hard work and careful planning, develop the technology and bring a new product to market. The first of these medical breakthroughs was a proprietary collagen pad used to stop bleeding in surgery.

THE COLLAGEN STORY

Development of Datascope's collagen product traces back to 1982, when the company acquired the rights to a mechanical heart valve developed by Dr. Diego Figuera, chief cardiovascular surgeon at the Clinica Puerta de Hierro, in Madrid, Spain. The Figuera-Datascope heart valve had a unique design

---

Datascope's logo went through a number of changes in the late 1980s.

that minimized blood clots, the major complication associated with mechanical valves.[3]

Later that year, Datascope also bought the rights to a new biological heart valve co-invented by Dr. Figuera and Dr. Jose Castillo, chief of surgical research, also of the Clinica Puerta de Hierro. The new biological valve was made of tissue taken from the pericardium of a calf and chemically treated to create flexible, durable valve leaflets.[4]

During its research on these artificial heart valves, Datascope began looking at medical applications for collagen, a versatile, fibrous protein found in the connective tissue of animals and humans.[5]

"Collagen is a naturally occurring protein," explained Patrice Napoda, senior regulatory affairs associate for Datascope's Collagen Products division. "It's in everyone's body, and it's a natural hemostatic agent, meaning that it stops bleeding."[6]

In 1983, after acquiring the rights to a new hemostatic collagen fleece (HCF), Datascope constructed a clinical testing and manufacturing facility in Holland and in 1984 began manufacturing its own creation of collagen designed to control bleeding during surgery. As Datascope explained, "HCF is a special aggregate of collagen fibers, in the form of a pad, which will rapidly cause blood clotting when applied to a bleeding surface."[7] In fact, part of the collagen pad formed a gel with the blood to effectively stop bleeding.

"The collagen is sourced from cow tendons and goes through quite an extensive chemical process to isolate and purify it," said Patrice Napoda. "Then it goes through a textiling process to create the type of fibers that we want to form."[8]

Trademarked Novacol, Datascope's biodegradable hemostatic collagen pad proved more effective and easier to use than other collagen hemostats on the market. Its long collagen fibers intertwined in a matrix, which kept the pad from tearing or opening the wound again once the blood clot had formed and the pad was removed. Though strong enough to take a suture, Novacol could also be cut, folded, and fitted around organs. In addition, it stopped bleeding much faster than synthetic hemostats and was far more effective than manual compression. The fact that the body completely resorbs and eliminates collagen after it has served its purpose made it even more appealing.[9] In 1985, Datascope began marketing Novacol in Europe, but it was still conducting clinical trials needed to get the FDA's green light for marketing Novacol in the United States.

Datascope's collagen processing involved a unique way of purifying and compressing long fibers of collagen taken from tendons of cattle into a hemostatic pad (shown magnified in inset).

The FDA gave its approval in June 1986. Two months later, Datascope partnered with Astra Pharmaceutical Products to market the collagen hemostatic pad in the United States under the trade name Astra Hemopad. Astra was part of AB Astra, a major European-based pharmaceutical company best known for its anesthetic Xylocaine.[10]

Datascope chose not to market the product itself because its direct sales force had not been primed to sell it. Saper wanted to keep the sales representatives focused on other products. Initial sales for Hemopad were promising, reaching $2.2 million by the end of June 1987.[11] But high inventory levels at Astra kept net income from reaching its potential,[12] and after a few years, Datascope ended the relationship and began marketing the collagen pad itself under a new trade name: FirstStop.

Still, clinical response to Hemopad was overwhelmingly positive. "The fact that it can be removed from the clot site very easily in one piece is a definite plus," said Kathleen Leone, a registered nurse with Hackensack Medical Center. And Sandy Caldwell, clinical nurse at Johns Hopkins Hospital, said, "I used Hemopad on a vascular case, and I was very impressed with the way it worked.... It seems to conform better to vessels, and it provides very good hemostasis."[13]

Also in the late 1980s, Datascope began developing a specific application for collagen to seal femoral artery punctures. Later, this research would result in another groundbreaking product called VasoSeal.

INTERVASCULAR: THE FIRST ACQUISITION

Around the same time that Astra was launching Datascope's new Hemopad, Datascope made its first acquisition.

Larry Saper had evaluated a few biotechnology companies for a possible acquisition but hadn't found what he was looking for.[14] "Datascope doesn't make acquisitions for the sake of getting bigger," explained Marty Nussbaum. "The company moves carefully. The transaction has to make sense. Datascope has to believe that something unique can be brought to bear."[15]

In the summer of 1986, Saper came across a company that truly intrigued him. Founded by Dr. George Goicoechea, InterVascular was a start-up company based in Clearwater, Florida. It manufactured a line of proprietary woven and knitted Dacron vascular grafts. (Dacron is a polyester yarn.) These synthetic grafts were surgically implanted in patients to replace damaged or diseased arteries. The product had enormous market potential in the healthcare sector, especially as the world's population aged at an accelerating rate.

After listening to Goicoechea describe InterVascular's groundbreaking technology for making artificial arteries, Saper was impressed. Here was a company, much like Datascope, based on an entrepreneurial spirit, innovation, and hard work.

"In essence, our company was a mirror of what InterVascular hoped to become," said Saper. "We saw them as innovators,

product champions with intimate knowledge of their customers' needs. Fundamentally, we recognized that here was something new and very promising."[16]

InterVascular had found a unique way to make these vascular grafts that made it easier for surgeons to preclot them. Preclotting the grafts involved soaking them in the patient's blood for 15 to 20 minutes before suturing them into place, a step surgeons preferred to skip since it took extra time and caused patients to lose more blood. Goicoechea and his team improved the design and manufacture of existing grafts by designing special weaving machines that added a patented Interloc cross-weave to the grafts. The cross-weave made them more durable and easier to graft.[17]

"Most wovens are made like a carpet," Goicoechea explained. "If you pull a thread, they unravel. We are able to interlock the yarn, which means the integrity of the graft is maintained, for example, when it is sutured.... Also, the Interloc weave won't ossify, attract calcium deposits, the way other wovens do."[18]

Datascope acquired 20 percent of InterVascular in September 1986, the same month that InterVascular received FDA permission to market its new grafts in the United States. (The company had gained European permission the year before.) "First, I wanted to watch the company," Saper later said, "so we bought a piece of it."[19]

In June 1988, Datascope bought the remaining 80 percent of InterVascular's shares, paying a total of $3.6 million in cash and stock.[20] Goicoechea stayed with Datascope as head of InterVascular, which was now a wholly owned Datascope subsidiary.

Saper's initial interest in InterVascular stemmed from his belief that Datascope's collagen technology could be applied to InterVascular's grafts. By 1987, that belief had become a reality. Working together, Datascope

InterVascular's polyester vascular grafts were constructed with a patented cross-weave, which is visible to the naked eye only when magnified.

and InterVascular developed Hemaguard and Poly-Graft, collagen-coated vascular grafts that eliminated the need for preclotting. No preclotting was required because collagen was naturally absorbable by the body and would form a gel between the patient's body and the graft so that the graft could be implanted immediately. As Saper explained, "Preclotting [uses] blood from the patient, an inconvenient procedure and often ineffective because of anticoagulants [substances that prevent blood clotting] in the patient's blood."[21]

In 1988, after leasing a 25,000-square-foot production facility in Clearwater, Florida, Datascope introduced Hemaguard and Poly-Graft in the European market while awaiting FDA approval for marketing in the United States.[22] In the meantime, the two new vascular grafts were selling well in Europe, thanks in part to a direct sales effort in France, where the grafts were partially manufactured, and in Germany.[23] In 1990, after the French government set up a *zone d'enterprise* to encourage new businesses in the country, InterVascular opened an office in La Ciotat, France, headed by Goicoechea, and received a 10-year tax exemption.

Next InterVascular entered the small-caliber blood vessel market in 1990 by introducing two new products: the Hemaguard RS and Poly-K RS. These were the first non-Teflon synthetic grafts for vessels.[24]

LEADER OF THE PACK

Datascope's efforts to advance other areas of medicine did not hinder developments in its older product lines. "Our products are always being changed, and they're always being refined, and new ones are being developed," said Saper. "It's a continuous creative process to solve new problems. There's no one specific direction — except as technology changes, those advances are incorporated into the particular products that we make."[25]

Datascope was the indisputable leader of the pack when it came to IABP (holding about two thirds of the IABP market in 1988), and the therapy was continuing to gain acceptance in community hospitals. These hospitals were often the first stop for serious heart attack patients, before they were transported elsewhere for surgery.

Dr. Vaidya, a cardiologist at Hackensack Medical Center, in Bergen County, New Jersey, which received many heart attack patients from Pascack Valley Hospital, a community hospital, explained the importance of IABP to community hospitals.

By stabilizing a person who's had or is in the middle of having a heart attack, a doctor is buying valuable time. With the balloon pump, you can stabilize a patient, and that lets you evaluate his condition and determine what treatment he needs in a way that you can't if he's in shock. It enables doctors to bring a person out of shock early, and that's important because if a person stays in shock too long, his organs can start deteriorating and then you can't use the pump or medication. At that point, nothing will work.[26]

Over the years, IABP systems had become increasingly smaller, lighter, and easier to use, making them more appealing to community hospitals. The first IABP system weighed about 500 pounds, and heart attack patients who needed to be kept attached to it on their way to open-heart surgery facilities had to be transported via truck because ambulances couldn't accommodate the pump. By contrast, the balloon pumps of the 1980s were much simpler to operate and about one-quarter the original size. And thanks to Datascope's innovation, the balloon pump could fit under a stretcher, making it easy to get into an ambulance.[27]

In January 1986, after three years in development and clinical testing, Datascope began shipping System 90, its next-generation intra-aortic balloon pump, which incorporated brand-new technology. "We went from discrete components to computerized equipment," said Bob Velebir, senior technical support instructor for the Cardiac Assist division.[28]

Velebir had been on every IABP project team since the Datascope 80. "With each new pump, there's been a dramatic increase in technology and performance," he said. "We've always gone forward with each new system. And there have always been three basic factors that are crucial for each new system: We make it easy to operate, we make it reliable, and we offer service. If we do find anything wrong, we always take care of it voluntarily. My ultimate goal is to make things better for the end user, who is the patient on that pump."[29]

NO STEP DOWN

Also in 1986, Datascope introduced a new series of balloon catheters called Percor Stat-DL.[30] The superflexible 9.5 Fr. Percor Stat-DL was introduced in 1987 and had the smallest sheath size of any dual-lumen catheter on the market. Catheters to that time were inserted percutaneously through a sheath. Although a balloon catheter might measure 9.5 Fr., the sheath had to be larger to accommodate the balloon wrapped around it.

Unlike previous balloon catheters, the Stat balloon catheters had prefolded membranes, which, according to Walter Kaiser, manager of quality systems engineering for Cardiac Assist, represented a huge milestone in balloon catheter development. "When I started in 1983, the membrane of the balloon was not prefolded and ready for insertion," he explained. "The physician had to go through a whole procedure to get the catheter ready for insertion by using a mechanism to wrap up the membrane. Then we were able to develop the materials and the technique to prefold the balloon into what was called the Stat balloon. When that happened, the physician saved a good 20 minutes on his insertion time because the balloon was ready to go as soon as he took it out of the package."[31]

Moreover, the smaller sheath size meant the IABP could be used in more patients because it reduced the chance of interfering with blood flow in the artery near where the catheter was inserted.[32]

"Retainers hold the balloon into shape," explained Frank Frisch. "That shape is maintained so that if our product is 9.5 Fr., it's 9.5 from one end of the catheter to the tip of the membrane. A lot of our competitors have what they call a 'step down,' meaning that the balloon is bigger than the catheter. ... If the balloon is bigger than the catheter, the puncture in the patient's artery is one size as you're pushing in, and when the smaller catheter comes behind it, you'll get excessive bleeding because you've made the hole bigger than it needs to be."[33]

Infants and children sometimes need the help of IABP therapy. Datascope is the only company to offer a full line of pediatric IAB catheters.

After the 9.5 Fr. Percor Stat-DL, all of Datascope's balloon catheters would be designed with no step down. "That's one of our claims to fame," said Frisch.[34]

An even smaller model, the 8.5 Fr. Percor Stat-DL, received marketing approval from the FDA in 1990.

IABP AND INTERVENTIONAL CARDIOLOGY

Meanwhile, IABP was taking on a critical role in the less-invasive cardiology revolution. One of its groundbreaking less-invasive procedures was coronary angioplasty. Coronary angioplasty uses a tiny balloon threaded through blocked arteries via a catheter. The balloon inflates to widen the artery and mash arterial plaque against the artery's walls, thus opening the blocked vessel. It provides an alternative to coronary bypass, which involves cracking open the patient's chest and stopping the heart. As one report noted, "Angioplasty was a quantum leap for cardiology, the doctor's first nonsurgical tool for intervening directly to prevent heart attacks before they happen."[35]

German-born physician Andreas Gruentzig had pioneered coronary angioplasty in the 1970s. Prior to that time, catheters had been used to clear clogged arteries in patients' legs and for probing coronary arteries for diagnostic purposes, but no one had yet tried to use catheters to treat heart disease. In the

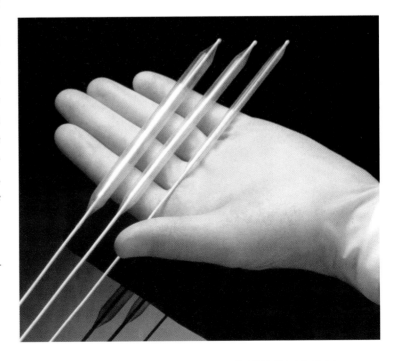

early 1970s, Gruentzig began fabricating his own balloons, which he attached to catheters, and practiced dilating the arteries of dogs and cadavers. He also began experimenting with his balloons to expand peripheral arteries in humans. Then on September 16, 1977, Gruentzig performed the first coronary angioplasty on a conscious human in a catheterization lab in Zurich. The treatment was successful. That same year, he successfully treated four other patients in Europe before sharing his results with the medical community. In 1978, coronary angioplasty was introduced in the United States.[36]

Other interventional cardiology research had shown that the heart was more durable than previously thought. Experiments showed that the heart muscle could heal itself after an acute attack if circulation were promptly restored — as it could through emergency coronary angioplasty. Other research found ways to dissolve arterial blood clots, a treatment called thrombolysis.

During the 1980s, interventional cardiology centers that used these new methods began cropping up in select areas around the country. The interventional cardiology center at Duke University Medical Center reported that interventional cardiology techniques lowered by 40 percent the mortality rate of patients who suffered heart attacks. About one in five patients referred to these centers arrived in cardiogenic shock (more than twice the incidence in community hospitals), so the ability to stabilize patients quickly was important.

Datascope's IABP technology bought valuable time for these interventional cardiologists to use emergency angioplasty and thrombolysis, both of which required the heart to be stabilized. Moreover, prompt balloon pumping after a heart attack could limit damage to the heart muscle.[37]

"I think that balloon pumping is ... able to improve coronary flow and potentially limit myocardial damage," attested Dr. Leslie W. Miller, director of the Coronary Intensive Care Unit at St. Louis University Medical Center. "When the cardiac muscle is failing significantly, especially due to coronary artery

Above: Datascope's 90T project team members pose with their creation, showing the System 90T's small size.

Left: Datascope's System 90T transport intra-aortic balloon pump was designed to fit easily into ambulances and helicopters.

disease, balloon pumping can help to support stunned or ischemic myocardium by augmenting coronary flow and decreasing myocardial oxygen consumption."[38]

Each year, more than half a million Americans died of heart attack before reaching a hospital. Unfortunately, most of those patients who would benefit from interventional cardiology lived too far away from interventional cardiology centers to be treated in time to save their lives.[39]

That's where another Datascope innovation came in. The System 90T IABP, introduced in 1987, was specially designed to be used in ambulances, helicopters, and fixed-wing aircraft so that patients could be quickly transported for emergency treatment and their hearts could be stabilized on the way. Dr. Richard Stack, Duke facility director, called the aggressive use of IABP a *"key* element" in changing the poor prognosis for cardiogenic shock.[40]

Response to the 90T was overwhelmingly positive. As Dr. Norman Snow, medical director of the air ambulance team at Cleveland Metropolitan General Hospital, noted, "The configuration [of the 90T]...is most convenient. It makes it a lot easier, a lot simpler to utilize, and a lot more compact. Much safer, too.... Datascope has responded to a need. It's a selective need, but for the patient who has the need, it is lifesaving."[41]

INTEGRA: THE FREE-WIRE CATHETER

Datascope's interest in coronary angioplasty led the company to develop its own coronary angioplasty catheters. By the summer of 1989, after almost three years in development, Datascope began marketing its new Integra PTCA (percutaneous transluminal coronary angioplasty) catheter in Europe.[42]

Dubbed the "free-wire catheter," Integra was superior to other PTCA catheters on the market because it combined the advantages of both over-the-wire types (which worked with an independent guidewire) and fixed-wire types (which had a smaller profile). Integra was smaller than any other fixed-wire catheter and had a built-in guidewire so that a physician could more easily maneuver it in the patient's artery via an integrated steering knob.[43] As one source explained, "A patented mechanism allows the guidewire to move independently of the balloon on the tip."[44]

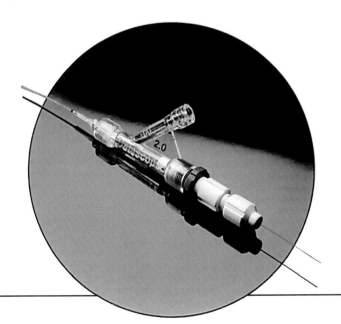

Integra was well received by doctors for its ability to reach lesions they wouldn't otherwise be able to reach. "The freedom of the Integra wire clearly makes this catheter more steerable or controllable than its 'fixed-wire' predecessors," said Dr. Pierre De Guise of the Montreal Heart Institute. "What's more, it maintains its steerability and control even in the face of complex anatomy."[45]

Dr. Douglas Morris, with Crawford Long Hospital of Emory University, in Atlanta, Georgia, agreed. "The Integra has an extremely low profile and exceptional steerability, especially in very difficult situations," he said. "Other products offer either tip manipulation or ease of crossing — but not both."[46]

Though the Integra combined the strengths of both fixed-wire and over-the-wire catheters, in market terms, it fit into the fixed-wire category, which represented about 20 percent of the total PTCA market. Next Datascope went after the over-the-wire catheter market by introducing Micross, which won FDA approval in 1990. The Micross-SL, a next-generation over-the-wire catheter, received FDA approval in 1991.[47] With over-the-wire types, a balloon catheter is slipped over the guidewire to be directed through the artery to the blockage. As analyst Mariola B. Haggar with *Investors News* explained, the Micross-SL "has the advantage of accepting any guidewire and thereby saving hospitals the necessity of maintaining large catheter inventories."[48]

MONITORING THE NEED

Datascope also added to its patient monitoring lineup. Staying in touch with the medical field's needs, in 1987 the company introduced the Accusat pulse oximeter, which continually monitored patients' blood oxygen saturation, was noninvasive, and provided accurate readings despite electrosurgical interference.

As Saper noted, "Oxygen saturation...is vital to know during anesthesia because it tells whether adequate oxygen delivery is being given to the patient."[49] If insufficient oxygen in

Integra, Datascope's "free-wire catheter" for coronary angioplasty, had a smaller profile than other fixed-wire catheters, plus a built-in guidewire and steering knob for easy maneuverability.

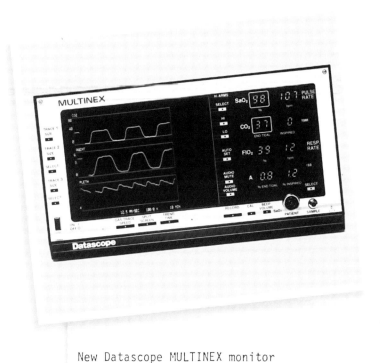

New Datascope MULTINEX monitor
displays CO_2, O_2, N_2O, SaO_2 and agent.

In response to a growing demand for more sophisticated pulse oximeters and CO_2 monitoring, Datascope introduced the Multinex, a multifunction monitor that performed both those functions while monitoring the amount of anesthesia in the patient's airway.

the blood is not detected early and treated, it can lead to brain damage and death. Monitoring blood oxygen level using the noninvasive pulse oximeter offered a simple, effective safeguard for patients.

The Accusat measured blood oxygen saturation by determining the amount of oxygen carried by hemoglobin in the blood. "By that measurement, you can get the percentage of oxygen in the blood," said Bob Terranova, director of engineering for the Patient Monitoring division. "Prior to this technology, they had to draw a sample of blood, take that sample to a lab, and have it read. That took at least 20 minutes to get the reading back. Now it's immediate and constant, and it's noninvasive."[50]

With the Accusat, Datascope now offered three types of noninvasive monitors that were especially useful for the anesthesiologist or critical care nurse: the Accusat (for monitoring blood oxygen), the Accucap (for monitoring carbon dioxide production), and the Accucom (for monitoring cardiac output).[51]

Also in 1987, Datascope released the 2200I, which combined noninvasive blood pressure monitoring with invasive pressure and ECG monitoring. The Accucom 2, a more sophisticated continuous cardiac output monitor, also made its debut in 1987. Two years later, Datascope introduced the Accutorr 3 and Accutorr 4, which combined pulse oximetry with noninvasive blood pressure monitoring.[52]

As operating rooms began to shift from single-purpose monitors to multifunctional ones in order to improve patient safety, Datascope responded and within two years had replaced its entire line of monitors with multifunctional systems. The Multinex, introduced in 1988, was a respiratory gas monitor that combined carbon dioxide monitoring and pulse oximetry with monitoring the concentration of anesthesia in a patient's airway. Multinex was the only monitor especially designed to be easily upgraded in the field. Moreover, said Saper, Datascope was one of the first companies to introduce an instrument that monitored all three of those essential parameters. Also in 1988, the company introduced the Datascope 3000, another multifunction monitor, which combined pulse oximeter monitoring with an advanced version of the 2200I.[53]

Meanwhile, concern about the spread of AIDS and other infections led Datascope to another product innovation. In 1986, the U.S. Surgeon General's office published its "unusually explicit" report on AIDS, urging parents and schools to start "frank, open discussions" about the disease. In 1988, as the global mobilization against AIDS continued, a world summit of ministers of health was held in London to discuss a common AIDS strategy. The summit, attended by delegates from 148 countries, focused on programs for AIDS prevention. Some 87 million Americans read a booklet by Surgeon General C. Everett Koop called *Understanding AIDS,* published in June 1988, making it the single most widely read publication in the United States.[54]

Concerned about the possibility of spreading AIDS by reusing needles and other medical products that came in contact with patients, hospitals had begun buying single-use oximetry sensors despite their high cost. To help alleviate this cost, Saper came up with the idea of covering the sensor with a low-cost transparent sleeve that could be thrown away after use. The Flexisensor oximetry sensor system was introduced in 1989. "Nobody had thought of doing it," Saper later said. "It wasn't a huge R&D expenditure; it was a case of making do with very little."[55]

Overall, Datascope's monitors had become essential to many anesthesiologists and critical care nurses, who used them to avoid risks. As Saper explained in a 1988 interview with *CEO Interviews:*

Making anesthesia safer is extremely important and bears very heavily on the liability insurance burden of anesthesiologists. Over the last three or four years, there has developed a tremendous interest in monitoring new physiological variables,

among them the oxygen saturation of the blood and the amount of CO_2 production of the patient, which gives the anesthesiologist a better handle on the respiration of the patient.[56]

HIGH RATINGS

Datascope's dedication to quality and innovation was rewarded by continued strong sales and earnings, and Wall Street was thrilled with Datascope's performance. In December 1986, the company's stock was featured in *Fortune* magazine as a "Big Board bargain," based on its high-output earnings.[57] And as *Investor's Daily* reported in April 1986, "With new products coming on the market at the right time, and an increased sales force to sell them, Datascope Corp. could be on the edge of a big burst in earnings."[58]

The esteemed financial newspaper was correct. In fiscal 1986, Datascope's sales jumped 33 percent over the previous year, to $67.4 million, and net earnings shot up 79.4 percent, to $3 million. Sales and earnings continued their rapid rise in 1987 with sales increasing to $87.6 million and net earnings rising to $5.5 million.

George Heller and Larry Saper (front row center) preside over a national meeting of Patient Monitoring sales representatives in Fort Lauderdale, Florida.

Groundbreaking ceremonies for Datascope's new headquarters in Montvale, New Jersey, took place on October 29, 1987. From left: Murray Pitkowsky, vice president of finance and treasurer; William Meister, president of Brown and Matthews Construction Management; Bruce Hanson, executive vice president of operations; Bill Terrell, vice president of corporate design; Larry Saper, chairman and president; André Cohen, executive vice president of marketing; Peter Marino, architect; George Heller, senior vice president; Joseph Grayzel, board member and medical consultant; and Ernst Janzen, senior vice president of international.

As always, the gains were a result of Datascope's new products and the rising productivity of its worldwide direct sales force. After a concerted effort to build up its sales force, by June 1986 Datascope had 81 sales representatives. And as analyst Bernard McDonagh, of Piper Jaffray & Hopwood, noted in 1989, "The company has a terrific sales staff. They service the hell out of people."[59]

"Service is very important," Saper said. "The key to doing well in the medical device field is to make devices that fill an important clinical need and that perform, but you also have to provide service — the physical service of taking care of the equipment to make sure it keeps working and the support service."[60]

International sales kept pace with domestic sales, especially after Datascope opened its fourth European direct sales subsidiary, this one in Paris, France, in 1988. For that fiscal year, international sales represented 17 percent of the company's total sales and had increased 30 percent from the year before.[61]

Despite the stock market crash in October 1987, Datascope's 1988 fiscal year was its "best ever," according to Saper. Sales were up 20 percent to $105.2 million, and net earnings rose 78 percent to $9.68 million. Despite significant start-up costs involved with the Integra PTCA catheter, sales and earnings rose again in 1989. Sales rose to $113.2 million, and net earnings increased to $10.5 million.

In early 1988, *Crain's New York Business* reported that Datascope was "fit as a fiddle." Datascope's stock, according to analyst Mariola B. Haggar, vice president at Prescott Ball & Turben, was "very attractive. . . . I believe the company should be able to sustain its growth momentum." And analyst Joel Zimmerman, with Shearson Lehman Hutton, added Datascope to his "best buy" list and observed that it had done a good job of controlling costs.[62]

Also in 1988, the Value Line Investment Survey, which looks for continued strong price and earnings momentum, rated Datascope among 100 companies expected to have the greatest stock price appreciation. Value Line said Datascope had shown "stellar performance." At the time, Datascope's stock was trading in the $45-a-share range.[63]

"I think this is an excellent company, with an impressive, bright management," said Lawrence Haimovitch, an analyst with Swergold, Chefitz, in 1989. "It's a good long-term buy because the company doesn't have much downside risk."[64]

In January 1989, *Crain's New York Business* listed Datascope as one of its "hot firms to watch," commenting that it "enjoys dominant position in its core business and has a history of active research and development with new and upgraded products constantly being developed."[65]

Of course, all this growth didn't come without some growing pains. "That was kind of a precarious period in the company's growth," said Fred Adelman, corporate controller. "We had to create accounting systems, procedures, policies. I mean, you name it. Nothing was computerized. We would get the orders in, and we had people typing up invoices on the typewriter."[66]

"It used to be a tremendous amount of work to get the quarter closed," said Gary Sagaas, director of corporate accounting.

"We did everything on green bar paper. And when we did the consolidations, we'd use the same green bar paper, and we'd be changing it so much that we'd end up having to put a piece of paper over the top of it because we'd erase the paper away."[67]

It didn't take long for Datascope to get its operating systems up to speed. Never stingy about investing in the company to make it better, Datascope was soon outfitted with state-of-the-art computers and systems, including an ERP (enterprise resource planning) system and LAN (local area network) system that allowed communication throughout the entire domestic organization.

THE INNER WORKINGS

No one could deny that Datascope was doing well. But Saper wasn't about to rest on his laurels. He wanted to make sure the company stayed on the competitive edge by constantly investing in R&D, people, facilities, and operations.

In 1986, Datascope gained one of the country's keenest financial minds with the addition of Murray Pitkowsky, who succeeded Stuart Levy as vice president of finance and treasurer. "Murray is well rounded in his knowledge," said Adelman,

who reported to Pitkowsky. "He has a feel for and appreciation for the operations side of the business."[68]

Then in 1989, Dr. Richard Piazza, a critical care–monitoring scientist, joined the company as vice president of new product development. Piazza headed up a research team to develop monitors at Datascope's new lab in Seattle, Washington.

With all the new products Datascope had rolled out, it soon outgrew its IABP production facility in Paramus. But rather than expanding or moving somewhere else, in 1989 Datascope instituted an inventory efficiency plan modeled after a system that had originated in Japan in the 1970s. Just In Time, or JIT, emphasized lower inventories and tighter production schedules to create a more efficient, less wasteful work environment. "Ideally," one article noted, "the operation runs so smoothly that each component arrives where it's needed just in time to be used." Workers who used to do one job on the assembly

This certificate of appreciation was given to Datascope for its contribution to the American Association of Critical-Care Nurses' annual fund.

Certificate of Appreciation
THE AMERICAN ASSOCIATION OF CRITICAL-CARE NURSES EXPRESSES GRATITUDE TO
Datascope Corporation
FOR YOUR GENEROUS CONTRIBUTION TO THE ANNUAL FUND
1988~89

PRESIDENT

EXECUTIVE DIRECTOR

June 30, 1989
DATE

line now performed a variety of functions, and quality control became an ongoing process. Moreover, the company could respond more quickly to unexpected demands. Only six months after Datascope implemented JIT, staff morale had improved, inventory costs had been reduced, and overall efficiency had been enhanced.[69]

To mark its 25th anniversary, in December 1989 Datascope dedicated its new, 38,000-square-foot headquarters in Montvale, New Jersey. By then, the company employed a thousand people and produced 14 major products.

HONOR ROLL

Recognition for noteworthy contributions is a welcome addition to any company's portfolio, and Datascope received its share of honors and awards. On May 15, 1989, the American Association of Critical-Care Nurses (AACN) recognized Datascope for its support of AACN, the largest specialty nursing organization in the world. AACN was established in 1969 to help educate nurses about the newly developed intensive care units, which later grew to be an integral part of emergency care. Debra Joseph, manager of Datascope's clinical education services department,

collected the award while she was in Atlanta conducting eight workshops on intra-aortic balloon pumping. Joseph was a featured speaker at the AACN Teaching Institute.[70]

That same month, Datascope was nominated to receive a 1989 SAMME Award for Significant Achievement in Major Medical Electronics in the category of Patient Monitoring. The award was sponsored annually by M.D. Buyline. Datascope was nominated for its contribution to monitoring technology during the 1980s.[71]

Of course, the most noteworthy honor is to be recognized by patients — the end users of Datascope's products. The company often received letters of gratitude or personal thank-yous from patients and their families. Therese Dudek, a Datascope sales manager, told of one such event.

There was a patient who was having chest pain, and he was brought to a small community hospital, which had a balloon pump, and that was an anomaly at the time because the hospital

To mark its 25th anniversary, Datascope moved into its new corporate headquarters in Montvale, New Jersey.

didn't even have a catheter lab or an open-heart surgery program. The patient was started on drug therapy and was not responding, so the doctor used IABP therapy, and he stabilized very quickly. They were able to transfer the patient to a tertiary care center where they did emergency open-heart surgery.

The patient's wife came to one of our meetings with him and stated that without the field support and our commitment and the patience to go to the hospital and make sure the balloon pump was placed in the appropriate area, her husband would not have had the outcome he had and possibly would not be alive.[72]

DIVISIONALIZING

In March 1990, Datascope strengthened the company's operations by dividing into five product group divisions: Cardiac Assist, Patient Monitoring, Collagen Products, InterVascular, and Angioplasty. By divisionalizing, each product group could better focus on research and development, sales, marketing, clinical training, and finances.

Murray Pitkowsky explained why divisionalizing was a good move.

The company was pretty much centrally controlled. There was a monitoring sales force and a cardiac assist sales force, but both of those sales forces and all the marketing, all the international business came into one marketing executive regardless of the product. Similarly, there was an operational officer who had responsibility for all the manufacturing and engineering regardless of what they were manufacturing. I was the financial person, and I didn't know how each business was faring. By divisionalizing, business focus of responsibility was more clearly delineated.[73]

"We couldn't get focus or accountability under the centralized system," Saper said. "Administrative costs went up as a result of divisionalizing, but it was necessary in this different, more complex, more competitive marketplace."[74]

Bruce Hanson, by then an executive vice president, was appointed president of the new Cardiac Assist division, and George Goicoechea remained president of InterVascular. Harry Gugnani, formerly general manager of Ohmeda Monitoring Systems, was hired as president of the Patient Monitoring division, and John Cvinar, formerly president of

This letter from the president of M.D. Buyline tells Larry Saper that Datascope has been nominated to receive a 1989 SAMME Award for Significant Achievement in Major Medical Electronics for patient monitoring.

the USCI division of C. R. Bard, became president of the Angioplasty division.

From many employees' perspectives, divisionalizing the company was a turning point.

"Culturally, it was very different," said Lisa Brischler, director of purchasing and planning for Patient Monitoring. "There were a lot of new players in our division."[75]

But as Gayle Carr, project leader for Patient Monitoring, pointed out, "The businesses really took off after we divisionalized."[76]

Fred Adelman agreed. "The personality of the company, everything, was totally different. When we made the decision to divisionalize, we suddenly became 'a bigger company.' Divisionalizing was a necessary change and probably the biggest [operational] change in the history of the company."[77]

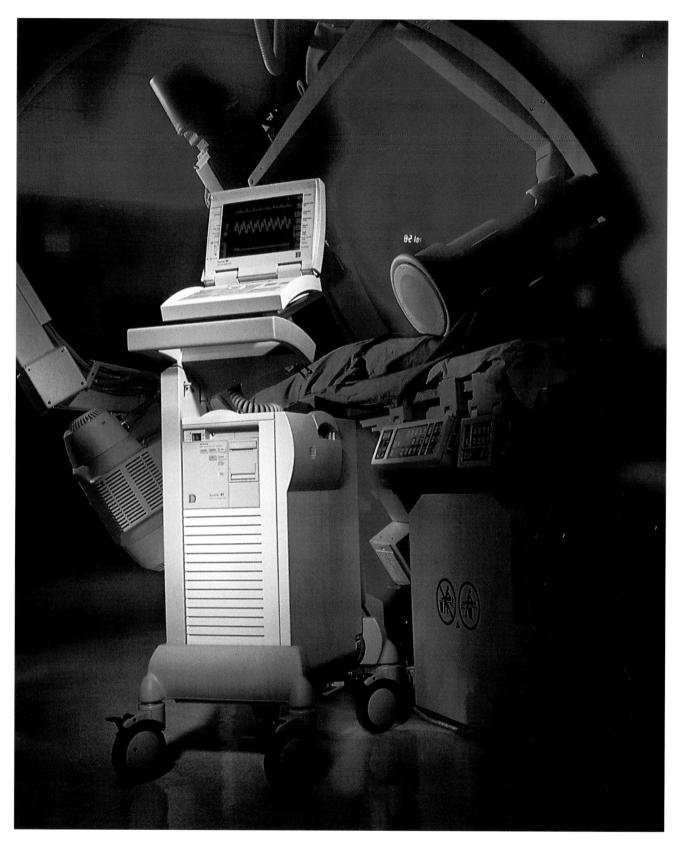

When it debuted in 1993, Datascope's System 97 "Small Wonder" was 60 percent smaller than other full-featured bedside IABPs. It incorporates a user-friendly and patient-friendly design.

CHAPTER SEVEN

TURNING PROBLEMS
INTO OPPORTUNITIES

1991–1995

We look for problems... because any problem is waiting for a solution.

— Larry Saper, 2002

THE 1990S WERE A DIFFI-
cult time for the healthcare
industry. President Clinton's
much-hyped healthcare reform plan
sought to overhaul the healthcare delivery system with
universal medical coverage. A rash of patient lawsuits throughout the decade caused malpractice insurance rates to skyrocket,
which forced physicians to charge more for services — an
expense sometimes swallowed by hospitals. Finally, the number of uninsured Americans who received healthcare services at
emergency rooms caused the overall cost of healthcare to rise
because the hospitals themselves often had to foot the bill.

And still the nation's healthcare needs climbed. As *Barron's*
reported in 1991, "With the aging of the population and thus
more use of intense services, companies that offer real advances
in medicine and ways to cut costs, such as reducing time and
labor by doctors and patient time in hospitals, should have a
bright future."[1]

Datascope was one such company, but as it had after
the Medicare amendments in 1983, it worked harder to
sell its products to hospitals on tight budgets. The fact that
Datascope's sales continued escalating throughout the decade
reflects not only on the company's dedicated sales force but on
every facet of its operations, from management and service to
clinical education and manufacturing. And as Datascope continued rolling out new products, its research and development
staff kept finding solutions to ongoing medical problems.

PUMPING UP IABP

Datascope's Cardiac Assist division
introduced a number of innovations that
improved its existing lineup. In 1991 the company began
marketing the sheathless Percor Stat-DL 9.5 Fr., the only intra-
aortic balloon catheter specifically designed for sheathless
insertion. With no sheath, the catheter took up 30 percent less
cross-sectional room in the femoral artery than the same catheter
inserted through a sheath. And because the artery was less
obstructed, complications involving limb ischemia, which
occurs when a portion of the body is not getting enough oxygenated blood, were greatly reduced.[2] The sheathless balloon
catheter was specially engineered with a stiff yet flexible
guidewire "to track easily through tortuous anatomy," the company explained. The vessel dilator was also newly designed, as
was the balloon catheter itself.[3] Later, Datascope would introduce
another guidewire specially designed for sheathless insertion.

The following year, Datascope unveiled the System 95
IABP, which featured a built-in computer modem that could

VasoSeal is yet another Datascope innovation. It became the first
vascular hemostasis device to receive FDA approval and created
an important new market for sealing arterial puncture wounds
after catheterizations.

send data from the IABP over telephone lines to be viewed by a physician or clinician at another location. This advanced feature was an industry first and exemplified how Datascope listened to customers.[4]

Then, in November 1993, Datascope's System 97 "Small Wonder" IABP hit the market. System 97 could be used at the patient's bedside or while the patient was in transit. It was particularly appealing because it incorporated advanced features yet was 60 percent smaller than any other bedside pump, making it the world's smallest full-featured balloon pump. System 97 quickly became the company's mainstay IABP system.[5]

"The goal in designing System 97 was to break the mold," said Nicholas Barker, vice president of corporate design, who joined Datascope in 1992. "We wanted to do something different, make it much smaller, and my goal was to make a machine that was thinking about the patient as one of the users. The person who has the longest and most intimate relationship with the product is actually the patient."[6]

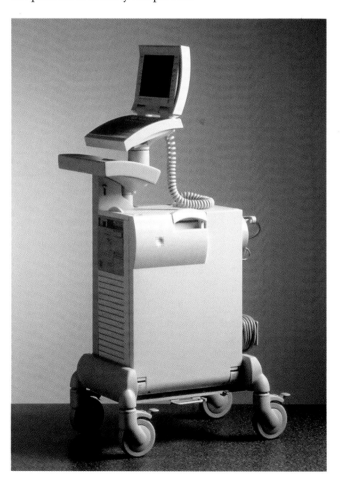

Barker explained that balloon pumps prior to System 97 were "tank-like machines. They were gray or varying shades of black, very hard-edged, very industrial looking," he said. "The goal was to try to make these scary-looking, life-saving machines more friendly looking, more optimistic, even in the choice of colors and especially in the choice of shapes."[7]

Barker gave another reason for making the balloon pumps look more friendly and attractive. "The product sits in the hallway much of the time," he said. "It's used in an emergency, and it's used a lot, but over half its life is spent, not hidden in a storage closet, but right nearby, where it can be retrieved quickly. It's like a little ambassador for Datascope that just sits there quietly year in and year out."[8]

Barker's role went beyond mere aesthetics. Ergonomics was also very important, and Datascope's machines were tested on real users. "That's the only way to really get it right," he said. "We test it, then change it, and test it again, and then do it again. The IABP is challenging because nurses must be able to use it easily even though they may use it as little as once a month. At the same time, it has to have all kinds of very high-level adjustments for a perfusionist, who uses it all the time. And then we have to design it with the biomed [technician] in mind, so we include onboard diagnostics and a variety of features that make it easy to service."[9]

Datascope became the indisputable leader in the balloon pump market and thus set many precedents in the pump's design and manufacture. "Because we were the dominant balloon pump manufacturer, the FDA looked to Datascope to basically be the company to help them define what the design standards were and what the performance standards were on the balloons and pumps," said Frank Casamassina, who came on board in 1991 as director of quality assurance and regulatory affairs for Cardiac Assist. "They spent a lot of time auditing us in 1992. When they finished what they were doing, they put a lot of requirements, a lot of responsibilities on us. We were basically the people they were relying upon to say how this whole industry should be run."[10]

System 97 was more aesthetically pleasing than previous IABP models. It incorporated advanced technologies and unique ergonomics to make it highly effective as well as easy to use.

Cardiac Assist's sales grew steadily despite more competition and hospitals' cost-cutting efforts. This growth was a reflection of the quality of the products as well as the company's clinical education and excellent sales and service. Increased use of IABP therapy, both domestically and internationally, also contributed to rising sales.

In 1995 Datascope introduced a companion tool for its IABPs called PC•IABP for Windows®. PC•IABP worked in conjunction with System 95 or System 97 (as well as Datascope's future balloon pumps) to allow Datascope's clinical service people to help healthcare workers who had questions or problems while using the pump. Deb Joseph, vice president of clinical services, explained how the PC•IABP worked.

If you're a nurse and you have a patient on the machine, you could call Datascope's emergency line and get a clinical person on the phone. The pump has a modem in it, so the clinical person could use his computer to call the balloon pump and, through the PC•IABP software, be able to see on his computer screen what the balloon pump screen looks like. So if the nurse was having a hard time managing the data or troubleshooting the machine while it was on a patient, the Datascope clinical person could see what the nurse is looking at to help troubleshoot that specific patient condition.[11]

IABP therapy continued to grow more prevalent, thanks in part to clinical studies that suggested intra-aortic balloon pumping might prevent most sudden coronary reocclusion (a partial or total blockage of a coronary artery) associated with thrombolysis (destroying or breaking up blood clots in vessels) and PTCA. Datascope subsequently supported a study at Duke University that found that IABP therapy significantly reduced sudden reocclusion in coronary angioplasty patients, some of whom had also undergone thrombolysis.[12]

A PASSPORT FOR PATIENTS ON THE MOVE

Datascope's patient monitoring line matured with more sophisticated machines that measured a growing array of patient parameters while continuing the company's tradition for ease of use. "We pride ourselves on making easy-to-use monitors with a very intuitive user interface," said Bob Terranova, director of engineering. "You can wind up with

two extremes. Either there are too many buttons, or else it's too menu driven and there aren't enough buttons." He said Datascope had cut this Gordian knot. "The most commonly used functions are available at the touch of a single key, and when you get into the more complex stuff, the stuff you don't use that often, it tends to be menu driven, so you don't complicate the keypad."[13]

In 1992, Datascope received clearance from the FDA to begin marketing Patient Monitoring's next breakthrough product: Passport, the first portable large-screen bedside monitor. Passport quickly became the company's flagship monitor, for it could be used in both the operating room and the emergency room.

Because it was battery powered and portable, Passport helped solve the problem of transporting sedated and anesthetized patients from one location to another. Passport had an easy-to-read flat-panel display, so it could be smaller than previous monitors, which made it more versatile, and its large display screen made it appropriate for bedside monitoring, too. The unit monitored pulse oximetry, noninvasive and invasive blood pressure, ECG, respiration, and temperature.[14]

Passport entered the market at a fortuitous time. The number of patients who needed monitoring was rising steadily as the population aged, and the growing number of outpatient surgery centers (also aimed at cutting costs) boosted demand. Furthermore, hospitals were trying to control costs by moving patients from individualized intensive care units to less costly units, in which multiple bedside monitors were linked to a central monitoring station.[15]

Passport was so popular that it cannibalized sales of Datascope's other monitors, but overall Patient Monitoring sales did not suffer. In fact, the division's sales rose 10 percent in 1992 and continued seeing double-digit growth over the next several years. The success of Passport spawned an entire line and allowed Datascope to capture an even larger piece of the patient monitoring market.

"Passport catapulted us into a whole new selling environment," said Steve Block, vice president of sales and marketing worldwide for Patient Monitoring. "It was the springboard to our [division's] number one position."[16]

In 1993, Datascope began shipping the Passport EL, which had a wide-angle, electroluminescent screen and the brightest display on the market.[17] That same year, Datascope incorporated carbon dioxide monitoring in a portable monitor with the Passport CO₂. And the Passport Dfib, also introduced in 1993, was the lightest, most compact multifunction monitor/defibrillator on the market.[18]

Datascope introduced some non-Passport monitors as well. The Visa Central Station monitor, which began shipping in 1992, could be linked to eight Passports via telemetry and helped hospitals maintain attentive patient care despite the ongoing problem of nurse shortages.[19] Point of View, the first critical care monitor

for bedside and transport use, made its debut the following year and was sold internationally.

INTERNATIONAL INTERVASCULAR

Though approval for marketing InterVascular's collagen-coated vascular grafts (renamed InterGard) in the United States and Japan did not come until 1997, the division's international sales were healthy, thanks to the ingenuity of the product and direct sales efforts in Europe. Meanwhile, the FDA cleared the way for one of InterVascular's other products. ULP, a woven, Dacron graft for abdominal and thoracic applications, began shipping in 1991 and was the first uncoated graft that did not require pre-clotting.[20]

THE MIRACLE OF VASOSEAL

Since physicians first began performing cardiac catheterizations, they faced certain problems: how to stop bleeding from the puncture wound that provides access to the femoral artery and how to deal with the puncture site so the patient could be moved, or ambulated. And since the late 1980s, Datascope had been researching ways to apply its collagen technology to solve these problems.

Dr. Andreas Gruentzig, known as the father of angioplasty, knew about Datascope's collagen research and thought collagen might be the solution to sealing the puncture wound. "He thought we could solve the problem," Saper said. Datascope conducted research in the United States, to no avail. Then Saper handed the research over to Ernst Jantzen at the company's clinical testing facility in Holland. "He came up with the solution," Saper said. "It involved deploying a collagen plug."

Thus in 1991 Datascope unveiled VasoSeal VHD, one of the most revolutionary medical device products since the intra-aortic balloon pump, creating an entirely new market for

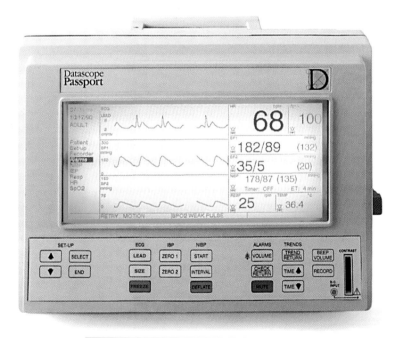

Right: InterVascular's InterGard knitted grafts are ideal for reconstructing abdominal and peripheral arteries.

Below: Introduced in 1992, the Passport monitor was hugely successful. It featured a wide-view, easy-to-read liquid crystal display (LCD) screen, and its battery-powered portability allowed it to easily travel with the patient.

sealing arterial punctures after catheterization. Both Jantzen and Saper's names are on the patent.

VasoSeal VHD became the first product to effectively cope with the arterial puncture wound from coronary angioplasty and angiography. (Angiography involved injecting dye into a vessel to detect blockage while angioplasty used a balloon catheter to widen blood vessels blocked by plaque.) By rapidly sealing the wound, VasoSeal prevented bleeding even when the patient was being treated with anticoagulants (substances that prevent blood clots).

Before VasoSeal VHD, sealing the puncture wound was awkward and burdensome for both the physician and the patient. After a catheterization, the physician or nurse had to apply manual compression to the artery for anywhere from 10 to 30 or more minutes, until a blood clot formed over the wound. Then a pressure dressing, clamp, or sandbag had to be applied to the patient's groin for anywhere from four to eight hours. The procedure immobilized the patient and was painful and uncomfortable. It also required frequent monitoring by nurses.[21]

VasoSeal eliminated those complications. As soon as they finished a catheterization, doctors could remove the sheath that helped guide the catheter and immediately seal the wound with collagen. VasoSeal delivered a proprietary, highly purified collagen directly to the surface of the artery via a specially designed plunger-like device. The collagen formed a plug at the puncture site, creating a secure hemostatic seal over the puncture.

"Collagen takes what the body does naturally and augments it," explained Rosanne Terraciano, senior product manager for VasoSeal.[22]

Or, as Tim Shannon, director of sales for Collagen Products, explained, "The tip of the collagen meets the arteriotomy, and once that tip of the collagen mixes with the warm blood at the site, it facilitates hemostasis and accelerates the platelet aggregation right at the site of the opening of the artery."[23]

Clinical tests showed that VasoSeal VHD stopped bleeding about 75 percent faster than conventional compression methods. Moreover, VasoSeal required only a gauze dressing at the puncture site rather than four to eight hours of sandbagging, clamping, or pressure bandaging, which immobilized the patient and was uncomfortable and often painful.[24]

"Prior to vascular closure devices, patients had to lie flat on their backs with their leg straight, not moving it, for four

to six hours," said Terraciano. "With VasoSeal, they can sit up, and that makes the patient a lot more comfortable."[25]

Furthermore, the conventional method of managing the puncture wound often involved complications that wouldn't occur if VasoSeal were being used. "We observed that when the sheath is removed, the physician must deal with a high-pressure wound," Saper explained. "This often presents a Hobson's choice."[26]

In angioplasty procedures, many patients were heavily anticoagulated for up to 24 hours to discourage blood clots from forming. The longer the patient could be anticoagulated, the less risk of heart attack or dangerous blood clots forming in the vessels. Unfortunately, anticoagulated patients ran a higher risk of bleeding around the sheath since it couldn't be safely removed until hours after the anticoagulation wore off. If such bleeding did occur, anticoagulation had to be stopped and the sheath removed. When that happened, at least one physician and an assistant had to apply manual compression to the artery for at least one hour to stop the bleeding.

"If the anticoagulation period is decreased," Saper said, "then the risk of blood clots and heart attack is increased;

VasoSeal VHD eliminates complications in sealing arterial puncture wounds by deploying a proprietary collagen to the outside surface of the artery. The collagen forms a plug at the puncture site.

Datascope enjoys a noble reputation both at home and abroad. In 1994, England's Prince Charles toured the U.K. office.

however, the longer the sheath remains in place, the greater the risk of bleeding around the sheath."[27]

VasoSeal solved this dilemma because the sheath could be removed immediately after the angioplasty, allowing the patient to be anticoagulated without greater risk of bleeding.[28]

HOT STOCK

Even before Datascope filed its VasoSeal premarket approval (PMA) application with the FDA, investors responded positively to VasoSeal's potential. In April 1991, the company's stock shot up almost 6 points on Nasdaq, even while Nasdaq tumbled almost 7 points, mainly a result of a weak medical technology sector.[29] In

July, the *Wall Street Journal* reported that Datascope's shares had "doubled in the past six months and nearly tripled in the past 12.... Datascope's stock is riding high on expectations of a new product."[30]

Many analysts saw Datascope as a bright spot on an otherwise bleak healthcare playing field. Marc Cohodes, a general partner at Rocker Partners, a New York money management firm, told the *Wall Street Journal,* "We tend to be skeptical of healthcare. But I'm a believer that VasoSeal works. I think it's going to the moon."[31]

Cohodes wasn't putting all of his eggs in the VasoSeal basket, however. "Mr. Cohodes likes Datascope's lack of debt," reported the *Journal,* "its history of growing via research as opposed to acquisitions, its management and the fact that company insiders have held on to their stock."[32]

At the end of 1991, Datascope's stock was hovering over the $100 mark, and the company issued a three-for-one stock split, sparking interest from individual investors. This was the fifth split since the company had gone public in 1972.

Original shares, purchased at $19 each, were now worth more than $600.[33]

THE SEAL OF APPROVAL

The road to getting the FDA's marketing clearance for VasoSeal was unexpectedly long and bumpy. In February 1992, Datascope submitted a PMA application, including clinical trial data, to the FDA. "While it is not possible to project how long the regulatory process will take," the company reported, "we are hopeful that the VasoSeal application will be approved in 1993."[34]

Unfortunately, the approval took much longer than anticipated. In 1992, Datascope was able to begin marketing VasoSeal internationally on a limited scale and expected to get approval from Germany and the United Kingdom by the end of the year. But by the summer of 1993, Datascope still awaited registration approval from those countries. It did, however, receive approval to market VasoSeal in Canada and Australia.[35] In September 1994, Datascope won a minor victory when it received regulatory approval from Japan, and clearance for marketing in Holland came a month later.[36]

In August 1993, Datascope submitted an amendment to the VasoSeal PMA, narrowing the approval it sought. Datascope thought this would speed up the process, but it did just the opposite.[37] One year later, the FDA responded to the amendment, notifying Datascope that it required additional information to support VasoSeal's "clinical utility." In other words, it thought Datascope needed to broaden the claims it made for VasoSeal.[38]

Finally, on September 29, 1995, more than three and a half years after Datascope submitted its PMA application, the FDA gave the green light for Datascope to begin selling

Datascope employees at the Holland office gather for a group photo in 1992.

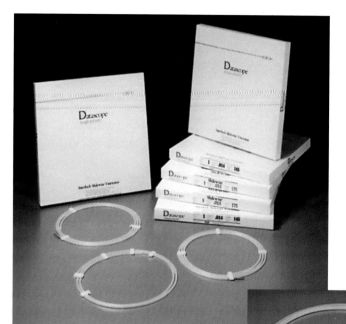

In 1993, Datascope sold its Angioplasty division, which included the Integra catheter (above and right), to Boston Scientific.

medical devices, but that didn't mean they knew what they were looking for yet. The industry didn't know what was needed either, and everybody needed to learn together. But by the early 1990s, the FDA had gotten ahead of us. I don't think we at Datascope had become sophisticated enough.[41]

Later, regulatory authorities would allow Datascope to put VasoSeal's other amazing qualities on the labeling: VasoSeal allowed patients to be ambulated sooner and thus leave the hospital sooner, which saved hospitals, patients, and insurance companies money. It also improved patient comfort and patient satisfaction and was effective for patients undergoing radiology procedures and receiving stents.

A CLEAN HOUSE

Datascope faced another challenge in the early 1990s. In fiscal 1992, it decided to suspend the PTCA division's operations, and in June 1993, it sold its entire angioplasty line, including the Integra catheter, to Boston Scientific. "At that time, we simply did not have the technology or the human resources to follow through and develop the line like it should have been developed," Saper explained.[42]

VasoSeal in the United States as a device that reduced the time to hemostasis in angiography and coronary angioplasty and allowed immediate removal of the sheath following angioplasty. These procedures alone represented a huge market. According to one study, in 1994 physicians performed 1.85 million coronary angiography and 460,000 coronary angioplasty procedures in the United States.[39] The company began conducting preliminary product training at a special booth at the American Heart Association meeting that winter.[40]

Arieh "Ari" Zak, who joined Datascope in 1992 as corporate counsel, described why he thought the PMA took longer than expected.

In the late 1970s, just after the FDA gained authority over medical devices, Datascope's approval submissions to the FDA were about two or three pages. Over time, the submissions have progressed from two or three pages to two or three or four volumes. The law had been passed that gave FDA jurisdiction over

Despite the multiple challenges Datascope faced in the first half of the decade, its balance sheet remained pristine. Sales continued their upward climb, and in fiscal 1993, earnings rose after two years of being dragged down by start-up costs from the PTCA division. At the end of fiscal 1995, Datascope's earnings stood at $17.3 million, an 11 percent increase from the year before, and its sales rose 7 percent to $195.7 million. It also stayed debt free and had working capital of $111 million.[43]

"Unlike a lot of other companies, our financial philosophy has been modestly conservative," said Murray Pitkowsky. "We do not rely on banks, and we do not *want* to rely on banks. As a result, we have an attitude that we're independent, that we will survive, good or bad, based on our ability to generate the cash needed to build the business."[44]

In 1994, the company replaced its Oakland facility after buying a 75,000-square-foot facility in Fairfield, New Jersey.

The new building housed the Cardiac Assist division and more than doubled Datascope's intra-aortic balloon manufacturing space. The Patient Monitoring division stayed in Paramus; the Collagen Products division shared the headquarters building in Montvale; and InterVascular was headquartered in Clearwater, Florida, and had a manufacturing facility in La Ciotat, France.

Datascope made some other significant moves as well. Richard Smernoff joined the company in 1992 as vice president of finance and treasurer, and Murray Pitkowsky moved out of that role to become senior vice president. Russell Van Zandt came on board as a company vice president and as president of the Cardiac Assist division.

In 1993, Timothy Haines succeeded George Goicoechea as president of InterVascular, Richard Monastersky became vice president of human resources, and S. Arieh Zak became the company's first in-house corporate counsel. In 1994, Barry Cheskin became president of the Collagen Products division, and Stephen Wasserman replaced Harry Gugnani as president of the Patient Monitoring division. The following year, Susan Chapman moved into the role of assistant corporate secretary.

SERVICE AND SUPPORT

Datascope's clinical education and service staff gave the company a huge competitive advantage in addition to providing a very valuable service. Customers who bought Datascope products knew they could count on continuing support from the company. "Datascope's face is always there," said Dottie Hanratty, manager of administration and customer support. "Customers know they can count on us after we make the sale. We're there to support the product after the fact, whether it be through education or through additional training or to do a repair or to deliver a battery. We're a constant presence."[45]

"Clinical training is definitely one of our strengths," said Tom Dugan, vice president of business development. "We do a very good job of training our customers, and they appreciate it. Because even though our customers are physicians and nurses, they don't always understand the clinical applications of specific products. Our clinical training helps differentiate us from our competitors."[46]

Dr. Joseph Grayzel agreed. "The clinical education and clinical field support staff is one of Datascope's biggest assets,"

he said. "Datascope has an outstanding group of people in the field supporting the customers in how to use the equipment."[47]

Providing clinical service was important for all of Datascope's products but especially for the balloon pump. "It's not used every day," said Tanya Fawcett, clinical services manager, "so it requires that we help nurses, physicians, perfusionists, and cardiovascular technicians to maintain a knowledge level so they use the therapy effectively." Datascope accomplished this by developing programs tailored to the specific disciplines within the hospital. "For nurses, we focus more on bedside management because that's where they are with the patient," Fawcett said. "For physicians, we focus on the indications, making sure they know when to use the therapy and the actual insertion technique of the balloon."[48]

Datascope not only designed its training courses for the specific disciplines within the hospital but also for the individual hospital's needs. "Even if a hospital has been using our product, if they have new staff, we will tailor our education offerings to accommodate that new staff," said Susan Spadoni, clinical manager.[49]

Such training sessions were predominantly held in the hospitals through formal, accredited classroom programs. But the training could also be performed in a physician's office or even at the patient's bedside. "Sometimes the customer just needs to know the differences from one model to the next or may need a refresher," said Gordon Dewhurst, clinical development manager. "When the clinical account manager or the sales account manager goes into the hospital to see people, a lot of times, just through their conversations, they end

Datascope offers a number of educational materials to its customers, including this CD-ROM on counterpulsation.

up educating the users, providing them information on changes in the technology, changes in the clinical literature, bringing in new journal articles on the latest research."[50]

Datascope used a wide variety of support materials, such as videotapes and instructional CD-ROMs, on everything from counterpulsation and operation of the balloon pump to insertion of the balloon. The company also held symposiums on the therapy and maintained a dedicated staff of clinical education specialists — nurses with advanced clinical care training — who were available 24 hours a day.

"Our field clinical people have a challenging job," said Deb Joseph. "Because we provide 24-hour support service, they're traveling all the time. But they're out there because they're passionate about the IABP therapy. They're working because they remember the first patient they saw on the balloon pump and how that patient got better."[51]

Joseph explained the importance of the psychology behind the clinical training.

The training certainly contains a huge element of anatomy and physiology, but almost bigger than that is the whole psychology behind the training. Intra-aortic balloon pumping is something I could explain in four minutes, but because it's associated with a very sick person, the clinicians and nurses have a tendency to shy away from it. I've walked into hospitals where the nurse says, "I see your equipment, and it makes my palms sweaty." But they know it's not the equipment so much; it's that the patient who's going to be attached to the equipment is probably going to be pretty unstable, very sick.

Our overall goal is to educate the clinicians so they're not afraid of the therapy, so they understand it and appreciate it as something that's going to make the patient more stable.[52]

In addition, Datascope trained its sales people and distributors in the clinical knowledge they needed to sell the products.

Datascope's service also gave the company a competitive edge. Datascope had service representatives all over the United States and also maintained an international force, so if a customer had a question about a piece of Datascope equipment, any time of the day or night, it could be addressed.

"Our primary objective is to satisfy the customers and meet their needs," said Dottie Hanratty. "We guarantee a two-hour response time and a 24-hour response time if it's

necessary to come on site. We also provide loaner equipment and rentals, so if something unexpected comes up, they can have the equipment they need."[53]

"All of Datascope's service people are trained in most all the Datascope products, and they do service on those products as well," said Warren Shoop, vice president of worldwide service, who retired in 2003. "We also have a tech support group that customers can call if they have a problem or question about a piece of equipment, and tech support will work with the customer over the phone to try to resolve the issue."[54]

Datascope ensured that its tech support group was knowledgeable about new products even before the products were introduced. "It helps that our tech support people are on the project teams when the product's being created," said Shoop. "They do the service manuals. They sit in on committees. Then they'll put together a curriculum, and we'll use that to train our service people. Then once the product is out, we'll put together a training program for our customers."[55]

Datascope's field service technicians are highly trained, and the company's quick response time gives Datascope a competitive edge.

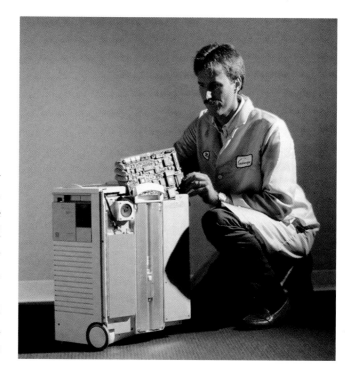

And like the clinical education staff, the service people showed their dedication to Datascope through their hard work. "When I go out in the field, I see these service guys, and they will just go nonstop, and they don't complain about anything," said Shoop. "They love it."[56]

RAISON D'ÊTRE

Saper believed that Datascope existed to solve problems, to meet needs. And in order to do that, the company had to understand what customers wanted and work to address those requirements. That's why building relationships with physicians, nurses, and other healthcare professionals was so vital. "Having a high-quality product is the ticket to the dance," said John Benkoczy, director of marketing for InterVascular. "But the quality is communicated to the surgeon through the sales rep and through the surgeon's knowledge about the company, through our reputation."[57]

Addressing customers' needs, said Nicholas Barker, is a Datascope trait. "There are a lot of things our customers want that pose technical challenges," he said. "Could we do well and not build those requirements into our products? Yes. Does it add expense to address those challenges? Yes. But we do it anyway, and everyone benefits."[58]

George Heller, who personified Datascope's willingness to listen to the customer and do whatever it took to serve the customer's needs, retired in December 1992 after 28 years with the company. He remained on the board of directors.

"George Heller is just a wonderful, wonderful man," said Susan Chapman. "He's definitely part of the heart and soul of this company."[59]

"George was always pleasant," said Mark Rappaport. "He never had an ego, was never snobbish. He was really the gentleman of the company, the calming influence. People throughout the organization loved and respected him."[60]

Heller was so well respected that Datascope's sales and service branches named an award after him. The George Heller Award is given to the sales rep of the year, the most highly regarded salesperson in the division. Recipients of the award are respected for their contribution to the community and Datascope. The George Heller Award is the most highly regarded award in the sales organization.

George Heller celebrated his 70th birthday on April 28, 1992. He retired later the same year.

Years after his retirement, Heller explained why he thought the company had honored him with an award in his name. "When I started at Datascope with Larry, I looked at the company as my own. I believe there's more to working than simply making money. If money is your object, there are a lot better ways to make it than the business I was in. But if you have a passion for something, if you really enjoy what you're doing, the money follows all the time."[61]

Heller had been Datascope's most senior employee and had served as Saper's right-hand man, helping to build the business, especially in the company's early days. The relationship he built with doctors, a relationship that he handed down to sales reps, was based on friendship and a willingness to help in any way he could. "Doctors knew they could call on me at any time," Heller said. "A problem is an opportunity to serve somebody."[62]

Heller taught well. That philosophy would remain a hallmark of Datascope's continuing success.

The ViewPoint central monitoring system, available in Europe, is designed to make the most of nurses' valuable time. ViewPoint was expected to be available in the United States in the fall of 2003.

CHAPTER EIGHT

PULLING AHEAD

1996–2003

Our goal is always to drive growth by constantly building a timely pipeline of new products in each of our four businesses.

— Larry Saper, 2002

THE BALANCED BUDGET ACT of 1997 sent the U.S. healthcare industry reeling. The act promised to provide the biggest investment in higher education since the GI Bill in 1945 and the most significant spending on children's healthcare since Medicaid was enacted in 1965. To reach its goals, the law increased cigarette and airline ticket taxes, but, more significant to healthcare, it also initiated cutbacks on payments to doctors and hospitals that provided Medicare services.

The chaos from these cutbacks resonated throughout the healthcare industry. The bill promised to provide more flexibility in managed care, but it also reduced Medicare's reimbursement rate to hospitals and other providers. In essence, these providers would collect less money while treating more patients.[1] As a result, many hospitals were forced to close or consolidate, and many others could barely stay in the black.

Once again, hospitals were intent on cutting costs, and competition among medical device companies spiked as they vied for a chunk of hospitals' limited expenditures. Several large medical device firms downsized to become more competitive, and others consolidated or formed alliances to maintain market share.[2] Even as Datascope jockeyed for position in the intensely competitive environment, its sales and earnings continued to rise, and it ultimately carved out a unique niche in each of its four product groups, a niche based on its commitment to developing innovative products that brought clinical as well as economic value to its customers.

A new slogan, written by David Altschiller, award-winning copywriter, chairman of an advertising agency, and freelance advertising resource for Datascope since 1970, conveyed the company's overarching creed: "Innovation is the best medicine."

CARDIAC ASSIST

Rivalry was particularly intense for the Cardiac Assist division, which had to contend with other medical device companies offering intra-aortic balloon catheters to hospitals free of charge so the hospitals might evaluate them. Rival companies also offered less-costly, less-sophisticated balloon pumps, forcing Datascope to lower prices on its more advanced pumps just to compete.[3] Datascope was able to

Datascope worked with anesthesiologists to design Anestar's unique ergonomics that make it more user-friendly than other anesthesia machines.

counter some of the competition by introducing System 96, a less-costly balloon pump, to the international market in 1996,[4] but the company still struggled to gain market share.

That didn't mean Datascope cut back on technological sophistication. The System 97e, introduced in Europe in 1997 and worldwide in 1998, was a breakthrough IABP and gave clinicians what they were looking for. The System 97e used CardioSync™ software to enhance its performance in patients with premature heartbeats and atrial fibrillation. It also had a built-in modem and contained diagnostic software that enabled Datascope service technicians to examine the internal workings of the pump remotely.

A new sheath called FlexiSheath, also released for the international market, boasted a wire-reinforced design that allowed physicians to more easily navigate it through blood vessels.[5] But perhaps Benchmark™, a PC-based database, was Datascope's

---

The System 98 IABP is engineered to be reliable even in the most challenging transport situations. It is small enough to be easily stored (left inset) and has an optional accessory storage case (below inset).

most unique product for 1997. Benchmark managed clinical IABP data so that Datascope IABP customers could compare their IABP routines with those of other IABP customers all over the world. The Benchmark database helped users of Datascope pumps achieve "best practice" of IABP.[6] According to Deb Joseph, vice president of Cardiac Assist's clinical services, 300 hospitals had participated in the registry by the spring of 2002, and Benchmark held 28,000 patient records.[7]

Despite these new products, the division's sales remained stalled. That didn't change until Cardiac Assist introduced two groundbreaking devices to the worldwide market, the System 98 balloon pump and the Profile 8 Fr. intra-aortic balloon catheter.

System 98 incorporated faster pneumatics, which controlled how the helium was pumped into the balloon, and proprietary algorithms to more effectively time the pumping with the patient's heartbeat. Such features better regulated the patient's blood pressure and were especially helpful for patients with atrial fibrillation or other irregularities of heartbeat. It also featured a larger, brighter display screen. The year after System 98 was introduced, sales of Datascope's balloon pumps shot up 14 percent.[8]

SIDNEY WOLVEK: A LEGENDARY MAN

ON OCTOBER 2, 1997, SIDNEY WOLVEK, one of Datascope's most beloved and talented people, died of complications from leukemia. Wolvek began working at Datascope in 1975 as director of advanced research and later as director of scientific research, but his contributions to Datascope and to the medical field in general stretch much further.

As an inventor, Wolvek was one of the greatest contributors to medical device development, especially in cardiac care. In 1967, he joined Adrian Kantrowitz's design team as a model builder. (Later, he specialized in building models of ironclad ships from the American Civil War.) The Kantrowitz team became the first to successfully use the intra-aortic balloon pump on a human. Co-inventing the percutaneous intra-aortic balloon was one of Wolvek's crowning achievements at Datascope, as was his contribution to developing a sheathless insertion technique for IABs. After meeting Dr. Andreas Gruentzig, Wolvek began exploring ways to seal arterial punctures.

But Wolvek's creativity showed itself in many other ways. He held 16 U.S. patents in medical devices and took part in numerous research teams that advanced medical devices. "As a resourceful, insightful, and unselfish team member, he was able to blend his own ideas with those of others to produce practical product designs, some of which have remained in use for decades after their conception," wrote Bob Schock in a eulogy to his predecessor and mentor.[1]

"Sid was the most influential man in my life," said Gary Schwartz. "He was a great mentor as well as a leader with humility. His name is still spoken with great reverence, and his inventions are still being manufactured and saving lives every day."[2]

Wolvek encouraged Schwartz to attend night classes to complete his engineering degree, which helped Schwartz progress his career, something Wolvek had done himself when he earned an MA degree in Interdisciplinary Studies from Brooklyn College, City University of New York. Schwartz also assisted Wolvek in building one-of-a-kind devices for physicians conducting research — a role he took over after Wolvek's death.

It seemed everyone who knew Sid Wolvek was touched by him in some way. "I worked closely with Sid for many years," said Walter Kaiser. "He was just an amazing person, the most wonderful person you'd ever want to meet. He was a fantastic engineer but had no formal engineering training other than the military. He became known through the coronary industry, even among the most famous coronary physicians, as an expert on coronary care."[3]

"Those of us fortunate enough to have known Sid knew that he was a great human being," Schock wrote. "He was a gentleman who lived his life with dignity, offering respect to all individuals. He also was blessed with a wry sense of humor and seemed to have an endless number of fascinating stories, but the story of Sid himself is one that cannot be forgotten. It is also one that those of us who are inventors of new medical devices will have a very hard time surpassing."[4]

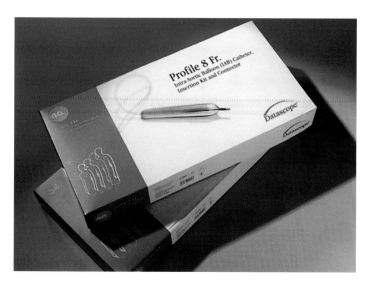

The Profile 8 Fr. intra-aortic balloon catheter allows cardiologists to move from interventional procedures to balloon pumping without having to change the introductory sheath.

"Customer enthusiasm for the System 98 balloon pump stems from the new pump's increased level of cardiac assist generally, and its unique ability to effectively assist patients with irregular heart rhythms such as atrial fibrillation," reported *BioTech Equipment Update.*[9]

The Profile 8 Fr. was truly the most advanced balloon catheter to date. Not only did it have the lowest insertion profile of any adult-sized balloon catheter, taking up 51 percent less space in the artery than the 9.5 Fr. catheter (when inserted without a sheath); it was also the only IAB to fit through an 8 Fr. sheath. The smaller balloon catheter made it easier for blood to flow through the artery, helping ensure that the lower leg was getting enough oxygenated blood. And because 8 Fr. was the standard-size sheath for angioplasty and stent placement, interventional cardiologists who did these procedures did not have to change sheaths if the patient also needed IABP therapy. The happy outcome was reduced chance of bleeding complications. Moreover, the Profile 8 Fr. had no "step-down" — that is, the folded balloon diameter was no larger than the catheter itself, so it could be inserted without a sheath.

Gary Schwartz, a research and development engineer for Cardiac Assist, remembered how development of the 8 Fr. balloon got started.

All the engineers were working on an 8.5 Fr. or 9 Fr. catheter, and Bob Schock believed we should be at 8 Fr. He came into the prototype lab and said, "How come you guys never built an 8 Fr. catheter?" I said, "I don't know, Bob. No one ever asked us to build one before." So we set to work in the lab. Two weeks later, I rushed into his office and said, "Here it is!"

Bob looked at it, and the next day he showed it to Mr. Saper, who ran it through an 8 Fr. sheath and said, "This is great! Make this project the highest priority." Within a year or so, it was out on the market. Nobody at that time had a true 8 Fr. catheter that went through an 8 Fr. sheath.[10]

The Profile 8 Fr. was extremely popular. In its first full year of shipments, it accounted for more than half of Datascope's IAB sales.[11]

Datascope introduced an even more advanced balloon pump in the United States and Europe at the end of 2000. The System 98XT used CardioSync 2™ software, which automatically adapted to irregularities in the patient's heartbeat, thereby making the IABP more effective, especially for high-risk patients. Its easy-access controls further reduced the amount of user intervention required.

Aside from introducing innovative new products, Datascope demonstrated that it was a cut above the competition through a campaign emphasizing its IABP products and unmatched clinical education and service. Another campaign promoted IABP therapy among interventional cardiologists in European markets. In the United States, IABP therapy was most commonly used with interventional cardiology, but in Europe it was mainly used to support patients in cardiac surgery. Europe presented a vast, untapped market for Datascope's balloon pumps and balloon catheters. More importantly, the company's efforts meant more patients would benefit from the therapy.

In the United States, Datascope continued educating hospitals about the benefits of early use of IABP therapy. Multiple clinical studies supported the idea that early use of IABP reduced mortality, complications, drug use, and length of hospital stay, especially for patients suffering from cardiogenic shock or who were about to undergo cardiac bypass surgery, angioplasty, or stenting procedures.[12]

IABP therapy got another boost in 2001 when the American Heart Association (AHA) revised its guidelines to include criteria for interventional cardiology procedures at community hospitals that didn't have cardiac surgery capabilities. The AHA also recommended that these community hospitals have intra-aortic balloon pumps on site. With about half of all heart attack victims in the United States being sent first to community hospitals, it was especially important for those hospitals to have balloon pumps so patients could receive early IABP therapy.[13]

In 2002, Datascope revamped the entire direct sales team for Cardiac Assist and outdid itself with the Fidelity 8 Fr. intra-aortic balloon catheter. "Every so often," the company reported, "a new product comes along that isn't a small step forward, but a giant leap ahead of everything that has preceded it."[14]

Fidelity incorporated all of the benefits of the Profile 8 Fr. with new features. Its unique polymer design allowed it to be inserted with less force and made it easier to navigate through tortuous anatomy. Once inserted, it provided physicians with extra insertable length to ensure optimal placement in the artery. Intended to replace the Profile 8 Fr., Fidelity was very well received, accounting for 20 percent of Datascope's IAB sales in the first full quarter after its release.

The creation of Fidelity exemplified how Datascope listened to its customers. "The Profile 8 Fr. had a smaller lumen inside it to make the whole thing smaller," said Schwartz. "Some of our customers told us they were getting a dampened arterial pressure signal as a result of that, which isn't good. The Fidelity has a larger inner lumen, and now the signal is much improved."[15]

PATIENT MONITORING

The Patient Monitoring division performed exceedingly well throughout the latter half of the decade as its

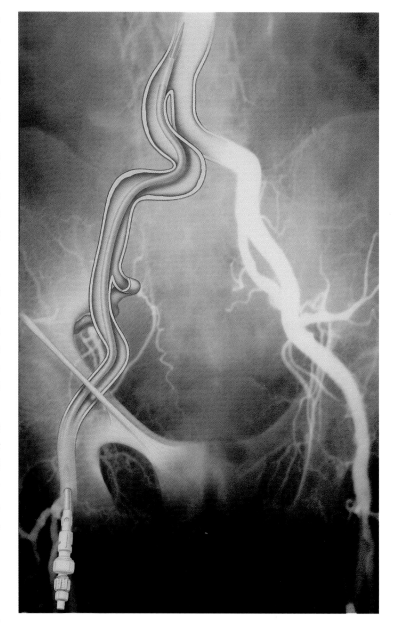

Above: This artist's rendition blended with a real X-ray shows how Datascope's balloon catheters are flexible enough to navigate through even the most twisted iliac artery.

Below: The Fidelity intra-aortic balloon catheter is another important breakthrough for counterpulsation therapy. It is easy to navigate through arteries filled with calcium and plaque and produces a clear pressure signal.

product pipeline regularly pumped out inventive new monitors that combined sophistication and pleasing aesthetics with user-friendly ergonomics. Patient Monitoring also beefed up its direct sales network and added new sales territories in the United States, thus reducing the amount of travel for each sales representative. The international sales staff expanded, too, and independent distributors overseas were replaced with direct sales representatives.

In the summer of 1996, Datascope began shipping the Passport XG, the next monitor in its highly successful Passport line. The Passport XG's screen was larger and brighter than other portable monitors', allowing nurses to see critical data from a greater distance. Also that year, Datascope introduced the Passport XG-CD, which made the waveforms more acute for improved viewing; the Passport XG2, which added carbon dioxide monitoring to the XG model; and the Passport XG2-CD, which combined all of these features.[16]

Like many medical device companies, Datascope formed partnerships that enabled it to compete. A partnership with Masimo Corporation, of Irvine, California, allowed Datascope to incorporate Masimo's signal extraction technology (SET) (for monitoring pulse oximetry) into its monitors. Masimo's technology for measuring blood oxygen saturation proved accurate even if the patient was in motion, and it was superior to any other technology Saper had seen. Moreover, an independent study presented in January 2003 at the Society for Technology in Anesthesia showed that the Masimo SET pulse oximeter "exhibited the best overall performance" compared to a main competitor's pulse oximetry sensors, "under conditions of motion, low perfusion, and hypoxemia in human volunteers."[17] The Datascope-Masimo partnership also allowed Datascope to sell Masimo's single-use sensors and reusable finger sensors.[18]

Masimo SET sensors quickly became the fastest-growing part of the Patient Monitoring division. "We originally entered into an agreement with Masimo because of our positive evaluation of Masimo's breakthrough technology and our belief that Masimo SET would eventually become the new standard in pulse oximetry," Saper said more than a year after the agreement was signed in 1996. "After working more closely with Masimo, we confirmed our initial conclusions regarding the clinical advantages of the technology."[19]

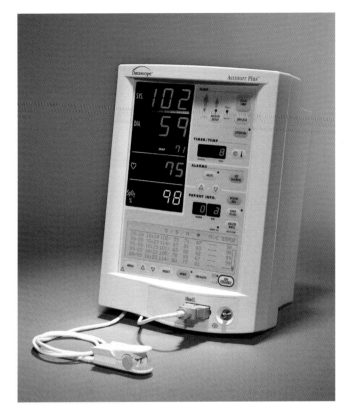

Datascope's Accutorr Plus noninvasive blood pressure monitor measures pulse oximetry, temperature, and heart rate and is available with a number of options.

Later, Datascope and Masimo teamed up to sell a co-branded signal extraction pulse oximeter called Radical, which incorporated Masimo SET technology in a handheld pulse oximeter. Nurses could easily carry Radical from room to room for monitoring patients during transport and for spot-checking oxygen saturation. It also worked as a stand-alone unit for bedside applications.

In 1997, Datascope partnered with another company, Tokyo-based Fukuda Denshi Company, to enter the high-end patient monitoring market. Fukuda Denshi had built up a nice position in the patient monitoring market in the 1980s, but over the years that market share faltered. Wanting to remain in the U.S. market, Fukuda Denshi redesigned its entire product line and formed a marketing alliance with Datascope, which

began selling Fukuda Denshi's high-end monitors under the trade name Expert.[20]

Launched in 1998, Expert combined modular design with the advanced monitoring needed in ORs, ICUs, and CCUs. The new monitor allowed Datascope to compete in the $350 million U.S. market for high-end patient monitoring systems and allowed hospitals to meet all their patient needs with Datascope products.[21]

Gas Module was introduced in 1998 as a companion to Passport to be used in the operating room by the anesthesiologist. It monitored CO_2, oxygen, nitrous oxide, and all five inhaled anesthetic agents, compared to only three monitored by Datascope's Multinex gas monitor. It was also half the size of the Multinex. (Gas Module II, the next generation, came out a few years later.) Also in 1998 came the Accutorr Plus noninvasive blood pressure monitor, which was ideal for spot-checking blood pressure and oxygen saturation. It measured pulse oximetry, temperature, and heart rate and had an integrated database that automatically recorded up to 100 patient measurements. The Accutorr Plus soon carried a number of options: long-life lithium-ion rechargeable battery, infrared or predictive temperature and recorder modules, rolling stand, printer module, and Masimo SET pulse oximetry.

In 1999, the Visa II central station monitor enhanced Datascope's product lineup, but Passport 2, introduced at the end of the year, quickly became the next star in the company's patient monitoring portfolio. Passport 2, like its predecessor, was a portable, battery-powered bedside monitor, but it weighed only 13.9 pounds, a full five pounds less than the Passport XG, even with an integrated power supply and advanced features. Also, it was designed to grow, to have different parameters added to it.

Passport 2's newly designed interface clearly made monitoring easier. "Instead of rummaging through the layers of menus, there's a unique Navigator knob," the company explained. "For often-used functions, there are quick-action keys. Waveforms automatically reconfigure when you need it."[22] Passport 2 incorporated Masimo SET sensors, and Oridion's MicroStream CO_2 eliminated the need for an external CO_2 sensor.[23] Over the next year, Datascope expanded the Passport 2 line to eight models, including a series of moderately priced models that addressed hospitals' cost-cutting efforts. It also created

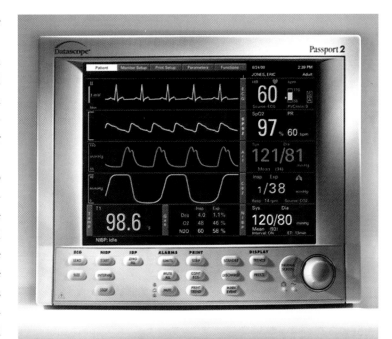

Above: The portable, battery-powered Passport 2 is one of Datascope's best-selling monitors. Its interface, which includes a unique Navigator knob and quick-action keys, is more intuitive for nurses than competitors' models.

Below: Ideal for acute care monitoring, Spectrum offers more waveforms, 12-lead ECG, and multiple invasive blood pressures in an easy-to-use, portable package.

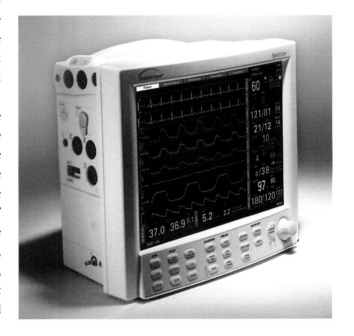

software for Passport 2 that increased the number of waveforms displayed from four to six. Another innovation, the View 12 ECG Analysis module, plugged into a card slot on the Passport 2 (and future monitors) and allowed medical professionals to view and print 12-lead ECG data.

In 2000, after the Federal Communications Commission (FCC) created the Wireless Medical Telemetry Service (WMTS), a protected radio-frequency band for medical communications, Datascope released PatientNet to replace the Visa central station monitors. PatientNet communicated patient data from Expert, Passport, and telepack monitors (worn by patients) to central monitoring stations through the WMTS band. Each PatientNet central station could monitor up to 16 patients. Another option let clinicians view information from patients in hospitals miles away.[24]

PatientNet addressed a growing need, Saper explained. "Increasingly, hospitals want to monitor more patients and . . . to do it at lower costs. The way to do that is to have one operator monitoring a whole lot of patients by means of a central system."[25]

The Patient Monitoring division found more niches in which to shine. In 2002, Datascope entered the anesthesia machine market with the introduction of Anestar. Crafted for the anesthesiologist's specific wishes, Anestar's ergonomics made it user-friendly, and its unique self-contained breathing system cut down on the number of connections needed to administer gases.[26]

Also in 2002, Patient Monitoring introduced a central monitoring system in Europe called ViewPoint. ViewPoint offered simplified menus, and its touch screen eliminated the need for a mouse, which helped minimize clutter at the nurse's work station. It also communicated with the Passport 2, allowing nurses to control common bedside functions and customize patients' alarm settings from the central monitoring system. ViewPoint monitored up to 16 patients and recorded patient information for up to 72 hours.[27]

Then came Spectrum, which bundled all the features needed for critical care patients — including more waveforms, a 12-lead ECG, multiple invasive blood pressures, a comprehensive calculations package, and cardiac output functions — into an easy-to-use monitor. A removable external module added extra-invasive blood pressure monitoring, cardiac output, and a second temperature port to

The ViewPoint central monitoring system has a touch screen and communicates with the Passport 2. It monitors up to 16 patients and keeps patient information in storage for up to 72 hours.

the Spectrum. "Portability is not sacrificed with the Spectrum," the company declared. "Lithium-ion battery technology gives you the ability to take all the patient's vital parameters with you. The Spectrum ensures patient care is not compromised or disrupted. No disconnecting cables, re-zeroing pressure lines or transferring modules to a second monitor — just take the Spectrum with you."[28]

Another monitor, Trio, was introduced to international markets in early 2003 and addressed those customers seeking a more cost-effective monitor. The highly versatile Trio combined all basic monitoring needs into a compact, portable bedside monitor that could be mounted on the wall, on the patient's bed rail, or on a rolling stand. Trio's small, lightweight design didn't mean it was short on features. It came with a color, four-trace display, a built-in alarm, a fold-away handle, and a built-in bed rail hook. It monitored blood pressure (noninvasively), pulse oximetry, temperature, and ECG. For more advanced needs, Trio could be retrofitted with Masimo SET pulse oximetry, invasive blood pressure monitoring, a lithium-ion battery, and a dual-trace recorder.

Trio was useful for meeting the short-term needs of outpatients, the immediate needs of patients in transport, and the longer-term needs at the patient's bedside. Susan Kaufman, associate business manager in marketing, said Trio had been "very well received. People love the fact that it's very compact, and it had a unique handle design where it's actually a handle as well as a bedside hook, so you can actually attach it to the side of a stretcher and use it while the patient is in transport."[29]

COLLAGEN PRODUCTS

Though the Collagen Products division continued manufacturing FirstStop, the absorbable collagen hemostat used to stop bleeding during surgery, it was VasoSeal that launched the division into the limelight.

For fiscal 1996, the division's sales shot up 62 percent over the previous year and an amazing 131 percent for fiscal 1997.[30] Sales continued to spike throughout the decade, and by 2001, Collagen Products accounted for 19 percent of Datascope's total sales.[31] Though a competitor came out with a vascular hemostasis device close on Datascope's heels, VasoSeal's sales and marketing

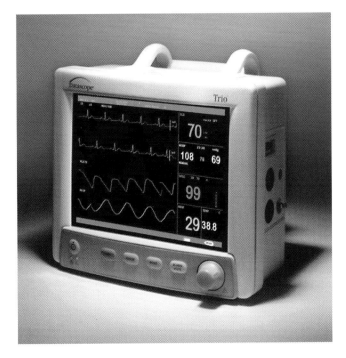

The low-cost, portable Trio monitor is designed to meet the constantly changing demands of modern hospital environments.

force, which emphasized clinical education and training, gave the division a strong foothold in the burgeoning market. Other competitors soon followed, but VasoSeal's sales continued to climb.

"VasoSeal's growth is accelerating despite strong competition," announced Murray Pitkowsky in 1998. "We believe this reflects both rapid growth of the market for vascular sealing products and Datascope's . . . investment in a greatly expanded sales and clinical organization."[32]

VasoSeal was able to increase market penetration and sales after a series of approvals from the FDA allowed Datascope to broaden its claims for what VasoSeal could do. By the end of 1997, Datascope had revised VasoSeal's labeling in a number of ways. First, patients who received VasoSeal could be ambulated much earlier than if manual or mechanical pressure methods were used. Early ambulation meant hospitals could free up valuable, high-maintenance recovery room beds by moving patients to less costly care settings. VasoSeal could also be used in radiology procedures and in patients receiving stents, which are implanted to support the arterial wall in conjunction with about 40 percent of the 500,000

Advertisements such as this one explain why VasoSeal is better than competitive sealing devices.

coronary angioplasty procedures performed annually in the United States.[33] VasoSeal was the first vascular closure device approved in the United States for use after stent implantation. In addition, VasoSeal increased patient satisfaction and comfort, especially among elderly patients and those with medical problems; no longer did patients have to remain motionless or lie flat on their backs for extended periods. Finally, VasoSeal was approved for use by nurses and technicians rather than just physicians — a reflection of how easy it was to use.[34] This meant VasoSeal could be deployed outside the cath lab, which meant quicker patient turnover in the lab. It also meant physicians could more quickly move on to their next procedure. And as Datascope noted, "Historically, nurses and technologists have managed puncture sites after diagnostic and inter-

ventional procedures. Therefore, it is natural for VasoSeal to be deployed by nurses and technologists."[35]

VasoSeal also increased market share by being *better* than competitors. VasoSeal was the only vascular hemostasis device that worked on the outside of the artery rather than the inside. With extravascular sealing, nothing is left behind in the artery, which meant patients experienced fewer complications. "Competitive products either deploy material inside the artery or use sutures that penetrate through the arterial wall," noted *Medical Industry Today*.[36]

Roseanne Terraciano explained the importance of not leaving anything in the femoral artery.

Patients who have heart disease are often back in the hospital for interventional procedures many times over the course of their lifetime. The driving factor behind our development strategy is to protect and preserve the femoral artery, which is really their lifeline to either diagnostic or interventional procedures. Whatever we develop, we use an extravascular approach. Say a patient has three procedures with permanent sutures. If you've left permanent sutures in the artery three times in the same area, you can imagine what the artery is going to look like.[37]

Of course, VasoSeal's extravascular technology was more than a marketing campaign. Interventional cardiologists, the physicians who dealt with patients every day, recognized the benefits of extravascular sealing.

"As an interventionist, I am reluctant to leave anything behind in the femoral artery," attested Dr. Barry Katzen, medical director at Miami Cardiac & Vascular Institute. "I like the fact that VasoSeal, in achieving hemostasis, delivers collagen on the extravascular surface of the femoral artery."[38]

Dr. Hal Skinner, of Central Baptist Hospital in Lexington, Kentucky, agreed. "I am reluctant to leave anything behind in the artery after the procedure. The risk of major complications such as surgical repair associated with using intervascular devices is just too high for me. The risk is significantly lowered with an extravascular device such as VasoSeal."[39]

In clinical tests that compared four arterial puncture closure techniques, VasoSeal had the highest successful deployment rate (97 percent) and the lowest major complication rate (0.6 percent). Moreover, VasoSeal was the only device whose major complication rate was lower than the 1 percent rate for manual compression.[40]

"Our overall complication rates [major and minor] with VasoSeal have been extremely low," said Dr. Jerry Glassman, director of cardiology at Mercy Hospital in San Diego. "We have experienced this low rate of complications despite the fact that we have been able to ambulate many of our patients in one hour. Our patients are extremely happy that they can ambulate in such a short period of time. Administration is pleased with the savings due to decreased observation time."[41]

What's more, because VasoSeal was extravascular, its effectiveness didn't depend on the condition of the inside of the artery, making it the only sealing device to be FDA approved for patients with peripheral vascular disease (vascular disease affecting blood vessels), a common condition among patients undergoing coronary or peripheral interventional procedures.[42]

Datascope introduced an improved, next-generation VasoSeal in Europe in 1998 and in the United States in 1999. With VasoSeal ES, healthcare workers no longer had to measure how deep to insert the VasoSeal device, thanks to its unique, temporary arterial locator system. Moreover, VasoSeal ES featured a one-size-fits-all (5 to 8 Fr.) design so hospitals didn't have to stock multiple sizes.[43] Once again, Datascope made the product improvements in response to customer feedback.

Unfortunately, the fact that Datascope had created a market also contributed to a bit of complacency within the Collagen Products division. "The division was so successful after creating the market, and it grew and grew and grew," said Jeffrey Purvin, president of the division. "It was giddy and exciting, and the division was growing so fast that there wasn't really time to imagine the day when competitors were going to make a difference."[44] In addition, he said, the division had a rather large gap in its pipeline of new products.

Purvin fixed the problem by focusing on market research — finding out what customers thought of Datascope's products versus competitors' products. The market research uncovered some interesting facts, Purvin said.

The great thing about our product is it doesn't leave anything inside the artery, and we were terribly enamored with that benefit — and it's a great benefit. Meanwhile, the competitors had products that left something behind in the artery,

and we just couldn't believe that doctors, who were, in fact, having serious complications, would want that product.

In the marketing research, we discovered that doctors don't like leaving something behind in the artery, but we had blinded ourselves to the benefits of competitors' devices. They operated faster. Also, our product required two people to deploy it. Yes, competitive devices sometimes involved terrible complications, but they worked more easily, more intuitively, and faster than ours did.[45]

Armed with its revealing marketing research, Collagen Products began focusing its R&D efforts on giving physicians more of what they wanted. Innovation is what Datascope delivered. In 2002, Collagen Products unveiled several new products and stepped up its clinical education services to further improve patient care — efforts that helped Datascope in the increasingly competitive market. It also motivated its sales force by restructuring sales territories to give all sales representatives an equal chance of making sales.

In 2002, as more patients underwent diagnostic procedures with smaller catheters, Datascope introduced VasoSeal VHD Low Profile, which provided a much-needed alternative

VasoSeal VHD Low Profile, introduced in 2002, seals puncture wounds made by 4 Fr. and 5 Fr. catheters, providing a much-needed alternative for patients undergoing diagnostic angiography procedures.

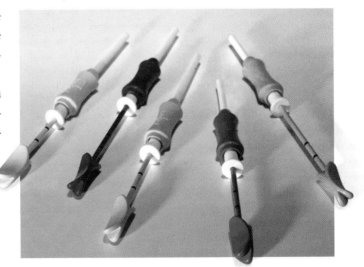

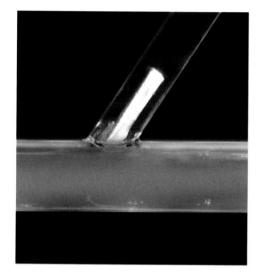 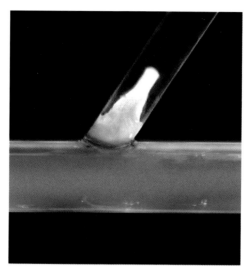 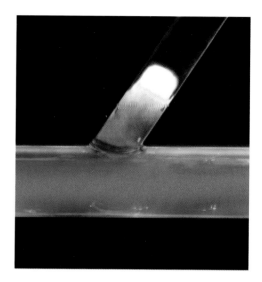

Above and below: VasoSeal Elite reduces the time it takes to stop bleeding at the arterial puncture site. It uses a proprietary hemostat collagen that expands once it comes in contact with the patient's blood. Moreover, VasoSeal Elite does not leave anything behind in the artery.

for these patients. Low Profile was designed to seal punctures made by 4 Fr. and 5 Fr. catheters, the size most often used in diagnostic angiography. At the time, the majority of VasoSeal's sales were for angiography applications.

"Low Profile is really a downsized version of the original [VHD] product," Tim Shannon, director of sales for Collagen Products, explained. "Downsizing is good because it requires the interventional person using the device to perform less dilation, which makes it easier to use.... Also,... there's less trauma to the tissue."[46]

In the meantime, Datascope was taking significant steps to move VasoSeal ahead of the competition. An improved deployment method called the Elite Technique was the first step toward that goal. In 2002, Datascope began retraining physicians and other healthcare workers to use the Elite Technique, which protected the mechanical seal created when VasoSeal's collagen plug was deployed, thus eliminating the need to put any pressure at all on the wound to achieve hemostasis.[47] Datascope expected the Elite Technique to "raise the barrier to competition in our user base," according to Saper, and early results were promising. VasoSeal usage at hospitals that switched to the Elite Technique was reportedly higher than before they switched.[48]

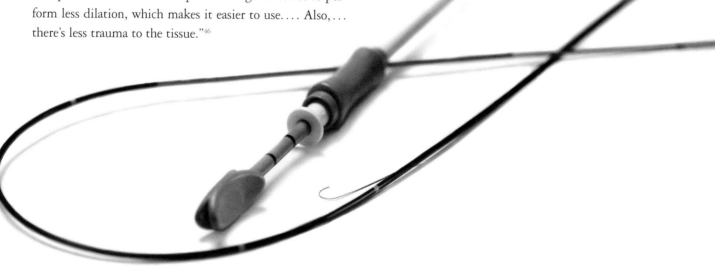

A second step in "raising the barrier to competition" came with the introduction of VasoSeal Elite, a new, proprietary collagen hemostat that significantly reduced time to hemostasis by further assuring an immediate mechanical seal over the wound. Some competitors' devices promoted quick hemostasis but left something behind in the artery. VasoSeal Elite provided fast hemostasis without that compromise. Once it came in contact with the patient's blood, VasoSeal Elite expanded to fill available space in the arterial puncture wound, even in patients who were heavily anticoagulated.[49] "Collagen attracts platelets to the blood," said Terraciano. "Anticoagulants prevent blood clotting; they're anti-platelet medications. For us to achieve such quick hemostasis time in this patient population is remarkable."[50]

INTERVASCULAR

Sales of InterVascular's InterGard collagen-coated vascular grafts and surgical patches continued to sell well internationally as Datascope awaited FDA clearance to begin marketing in the United States and Japan. The go-ahead from both countries came in 1997, just as InterVascular introduced a string of new products.

The InterGard Heparin graft, introduced in Europe in 1998 and the United States in 2001, became the first vascular graft that incorporated a drug to be approved by the FDA. InterVascular pioneered the concept of bonding heparin molecules to polyester, which resulted in the InterGard Heparin line of collagen grafts. Heparin is a naturally occurring substance that prolongs the clotting time of blood by discouraging fibrin from forming. It thus reduces the development of blood clots, which are associated with high risk of limb loss.

"Heparin is commonly used in medical practice to decrease the clotting of blood," explained John Benkoczy, director of marketing for InterVascular's U.S. operations. "One of the causes of failure of the vascular graft is they clot off. So heparin helps prevent that from happening."[51]

A polyester graft, InterGard Heparin demonstrated improved patient outcomes compared to small-caliber grafts made of PTFE material (primarily Teflon), which in 2001 dominated the small-caliber vascular graft market.[52] A number of studies had been done comparing polyester and PTFE grafts, and there seemed to be few differences in terms of quality and reliability, said Sean McNerney, InterVascular's vice president of sales and marketing. However, he said, the polyester grafts were easier to handle and caused less bleeding when they were sutured.[53]

The InterGard Heparin innovation came on top of InterVascular's other successful products: InterGard UltraThin grafts, made of the thinnest wall polyester vascular reconstructive product available; InterGard

Above: InterGard Heparin offers an innovative biological approach to vascular reconstruction by bonding heparin molecules to the graft. InterGard Heparin vascular grafts greatly reduce the chance of blood clots forming after implantation.

Below: InterGard Silver and InterGard Silver UltraThin (pictured) are the world's only antimicrobial vascular grafts. They incorporate the anti-infective properties of silver to stop infections from forming and spreading to surrounding tissue.

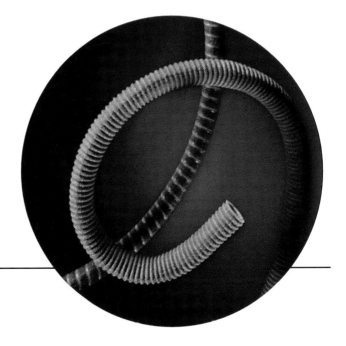

THE REGULATORY PROCESS

TRADITIONALLY, DATASCOPE INTRO-
duces its products in European markets before
marketing them in the United States. This is
largely due to differences in European and U.S. regulatory
approval processes.

"For the most part, it takes longer to get devices
approved in the United States because the international
countries tend to fall into a couple of categories,"
explained Ari Zak. "You have Europe, which has
largely privatized the approval process, so you don't
work with the government. You work with private
companies that have been certified by the governments
to do product review work for device companies. They
tend to move more quickly because their customers are
the device companies."[1]

Products that bear the "CE mark," the European
Community's regulatory stamp of approval (CE stands for
Communaute Europeanne), comply with the essential safety
requirements of the European Community and can be
marketed within most European countries.[2] Having a CE
mark for multiple European countries made the process
much faster than seeking regulatory approval in each
individual country.

Datascope's manufacturing facilities are required
to hold ISO 9001 certification, which the International
Standards Organization awards to companies that
meet its stringent quality standards guidelines.[3]

"Getting the CE mark is a two-step process," said
Patrice Napoda, senior regulatory affairs associate for
Collagen Products. "First, you have to get the manufacturing side certified. Then there's a paper submission,
which goes to your notified body."[4]

Japan, one of Datascope's major markets, has a distinctive regulatory process. According to Gary Mohr,
attorney for patents and regulatory, applications must be
submitted to the Ministry of Health. "Of course, getting
approval in the United States first helps," he said, "but it's
no guarantee. A lot of times, it's better to go through a
company that's based in Japan because they like to deal
with their own people."[5]

Gaining regulatory approval tends to be easiest in
Third World countries, Zak said. "For the most part, they
follow the lead of the United States. They assume the bar
is pretty high here, and it is. The FDA tends to be very conservative." After all, Zak said, "If the FDA approves a product that turns out to be unsafe, it's very visible, whereas the

Knitted grafts (small-caliber grafts), which could be
used in most abdominal and peripheral artery recon-
structions; and InterGard Woven grafts (large-caliber
grafts), which were designed for repairing thoracic
arteries and in open-heart surgery. InterVascular's line
of vascular patches included the HemaCarotid patch,
used for carotid endarterectomy and angioplasty; the
HemaPatch Knitted patch, used for angioplasty or
profundaplasty, and the HemaCarotid UltraThin
patch, which was easier to handle and suture than
other patches.

Next came InterGard Silver, the first graft to use an
antimicrobial agent to reduce the chance of infection after the
graft is implanted. InterVascular developed the device in

response to requests from the medical community for a product that would help minimize risk of infection.[54]

Silver is a natural anti-infective agent, and the
silver-coated grafts protect the surrounding tissue
after the graft is placed. This innovation was a major
breakthrough in the development of artificial grafts,
since anywhere from 1 to 6 percent of all artificial
graft implantations resulted in infection to the surrounding tissue. Such infections are very serious;
many patients die as a result, and many others must
have the infected limb amputated. Less important
than the patient's suffering but still a significant consideration, patients who experienced such infections
had to stay in the hospital for an average of 50 days

effect of delaying good products by six months to make doubly sure they're safe is generally invisible."[6]

Dealing with the FDA got somewhat easier in the mid-1990s, when the FDA issued guidance documents to help the industry determine whether a regulatory submission was even required. "Before then," said Zak, "the regulatory language was very vague; it said something to the effect that a change that could affect the safety or effectiveness of the device must be submitted as a new submission. Well, hypothetically, anything could affect the safety or effectiveness, so essentially everything had to be submitted. The FDA realized that they didn't need to see about half or three-quarters of these submissions coming in. So they did a lot of work and generated guidelines with some really useful flow charts to help you determine whether or not you have to make a submission."[7]

The new FDA guidelines encouraged progress by allowing companies like Datascope to make small improvements to products without months or years of delay. The guidelines also allowed medical device companies to make submissions more comprehensive. "We can give a lot more attention to each one because we're not doing nearly so many," Zak said. "The submissions have gotten better, and we're getting them through faster because they're better quality."[8]

Another welcome regulatory change came in 2003. The American healthcare system was in the midst of major change. Rising healthcare costs, propelled by cutbacks in HMO and Medicare benefits, continued to threaten the quality of healthcare. Rising out-of-pocket fees for patients and hospitals, escalating costs for prescription drugs, and longer hospital waiting lists also threatened quality patient care. Even the FDA, whose edict was to protect the consumer, was unintentionally hindering quality patient care through unnecessarily burdensome restrictions to the regulatory approval process.[9]

That began to change on January 31, 2003, when the FDA announced it would help make "innovative medical technologies available sooner" and would reduce the costs of developing safe and effective medical products while maintaining FDA's traditional high standards of consumer protection. The FDA planned to achieve all this by avoiding multiple cycles of FDA review whenever possible, adopting a quality systems approach to medical product reviews, and providing clearer guidance for particular diseases and technologies.[10]

The FDA's announcement was welcome news for medical device companies like Datascope. "The medical device industry is about as demanding an industry as you can find," Saper observed. "Aside from the usual demands of any industrial activity, the medical device industry is technologically diverse, highly competitive, and regulated by governments here and abroad."[11]

longer than they normally would. Such prolonged hospital stays drove up costs.[55]

Datascope began marketing InterGard Silver in Europe in 1999. Two years later, InterVascular launched InterGard Silver UltraThin to international markets. This second-generation InterGard Silver incorporated the thinnest knitted polyester collagen-coated graft on the market, which made it easier to handle. It also conformed better to the artery to which it was being grafted and simulated the patient's natural blood vessels by expanding and contracting with the patient's blood flow.[56]

More innovative products soon followed. The InterGard Aortic Arch and InterGard Hemabridge, two specialty grafts for repairing and replacing thoracic arteries,

received FDA clearance in the spring of 2002. Aortic Arch grafts had also proven effective in treating aortic arch aneurysm and total aortic arch replacement. "A special characteristic of the InterGard Aortic Arch Branched Graft as compared with other commercially available grafts is the anatomically correct angle of its branches," reported one clinical study. "[This] allows an easy suturing to the host vessels and prevents kinking of the branches."[57]

CLOSING CLEARWATER

In the meantime, InterVascular was making some other moves as well. In the fall of 2000, InterVascular ended operations at its leased manufacturing facility in

Clearwater, Florida, and moved everything to the newly expanded facility in La Ciotat, France. The cost of maintaining two plants was the main reason for the move, according to InterVascular's director of finance Anne Cuny, who took part in the decision making.[58]

Shutting down operations in Clearwater and moving everything to France made business sense, but it wasn't an easy decision. "We were very up front with the workforce in Clearwater as we were going through the decision process," said James Cooper, vice president of human resources. "That way it wasn't as much of a shock to people."

Characteristic of Datascope, Cooper sent an HR manager to Clearwater to make sure the workers were given "the best support they could be given," he said. "That meant separation packages, finding new employment. We even brought in other employers in the area to our facility to interview people during the transition phase. We were very successful in placing a lot of people with other companies before they even left."[59]

GOING DIRECT

Then, in January 2002, Datascope ended its relationship with Impra (a division of C. R. Bard), its InterVascular distributor, and began selling InterVascular products through its own direct sales force in the United States. "Based on the success of our direct sales model in France and Germany, we felt the U.S. market was a natural for us to invest in direct distribution," said Saper.[60]

Once again, the decision was difficult but necessary, for having its own direct U.S. sales force gave Datascope unrestricted access to market InterVascular products in the United States for the first time. This was a huge benefit for customers, who received better product support as a result. And buying directly from the manufacturer allowed customers to give feedback more easily, which in turn led to product enhancements that customers wanted.

The transition was challenging because Datascope suddenly went from having one customer to having 900 customers. Setting up internal systems was also challenging, but by the spring of 2002, the company had smoothed out most of the snags.[61]

"We've done well because we leverage off of Datascope's excellent reputation, and we position ourselves with our customers as a partner in technology," said Sean McNerney. A prime example of InterVascular's focus on technology was the heparin graft, he said. "We're putting more R&D investment into vascular grafts."[62]

GENISPHERE

In 1998, Datascope formed a new subsidiary called Genisphere to manufacture and market a new, proprietary class of three-dimensional DNA-based reagents (biologically or chemically active substances) used to detect and measure other biological substances. Life science researchers could use Genisphere's 3DNA to more easily detect genetic material such as DNA and proteins. "3DNA is a fitting name," explained Adam Saper, who joined the Genisphere team in 2001. "It's a DNA molecule that has tree-like branches. The sequence on the ends of those branches stick to what we're looking for. So if you were looking for a particular gene, for example, you would add a DNA sequence to the 3DNA molecule that would capture that particular gene to create a strong detection label."[63]

By 1997, 3DNA-based reagents had already been used to detect plant, animal, bacterial, and viral genes, including HIV and the Epstein-Barr virus.[64]

Genisphere focused on developing 3DNA-based products that improved performance of the new technologies used by major academic institutions and pharmaceutical and biotech industries to discover new drugs. The first Genisphere products aimed at drug discovery were fluorescent probes designed to improve the sensitivity and reliability of microarrays, an increasingly prevalent research tool used to detect nucleic acid, or RNA. The 3DNA molecule consists of a three-dimensional matrix of double-stranded DNA that is able to support hundreds of detection label molecules and which amplifies the sensitivity of the detection system.

Many researchers relied on Genisphere's 3DNA reagents to label RNA samples because they made microarray experiments more accurate. Researchers also liked 3DNA because it reduced the number of unknown variables in microarray experiments, an important consideration in scientific research. What's more, 3DNA was able to produce results with degraded RNA samples.[65]

Genisphere exemplified Datascope's commitment to finding solutions to medical problems. To help grow the new business, Datascope acquired Pennsylvania-based Polyprobe, Inc., the company that developed the 3DNA technology with Datascope's funding. Thor Nilsen, who founded Polyprobe, joined Genisphere as vice president for technology.[66] Genisphere originally operated out of Oakland, New Jersey, but relocated to Hatfield, Pennsylvania, in 2000, after the Oakland facility was sold.

REALIGNMENT

Some of the other Datascope divisions were relocating, too. The Collagen Products division soon outgrew its allotted space in Montvale, and in 2000 moved to a 90,000-square-foot facility in Mahwah, New Jersey, just a 15 minute drive from the corporate headquarters. (The Mahwah building also became home to Cardiac Assist's national distribution center.) That same year, the Patient Monitoring division moved from its two old buildings in Paramus to a newly constructed, company-owned 135,000-square-foot facility in Mahwah, just down the street from Collagen Products' new building. Patient Monitoring's manufacturing facility also produced Cardiac Assist's balloon pump systems. The VasoSeal manufacturing operations in the Netherlands were also closed, and all operations were moved to Mahwah.

In the meantime, Saper was strengthening his management team by shuffling seasoned veterans to new positions and hiring a handful of experienced people to fill top positions.

By 2002, the realignment was complete, with Larry Saper overseeing all the Datascope divisions and subsidiaries as chairman and CEO. Murray Pitkowsky, Saper's right-hand man, served as senior vice president, secretary, and CFO. Jeffrey Purvin, former vice president and general manager for Block Drug Company's Oral Health Care division, joined Datascope in 2001 as Collagen Products' president. Donald Southard, formerly vice president of sales, was promoted in 1997 to president of Patient Monitoring. Paul Southworth came on board in 1999 as president of Cardiac Assist, and Thomas Dugan stood in as president of InterVascular in addition to his duties as Datascope's vice president of business development.

Each division president was also a Datascope vice president, as were Nicholas Barker, vice president of corporate design; James Cooper, vice president of human resources; and Ari Zak, vice president of regulatory affairs and corporate counsel. Other executives included Fred Adelman, chief accounting officer and corporate controller; Susan Chapman, assistant secretary, and Frank Gutworth, assistant treasurer.

In 2002, Datascope also realigned its board of directors to increase the proportion of independent directors. For that reason, Dr. Joseph Grayzel, who had served on the board as Datascope's medical advisor since 1969, did not stand for reelection.

Above: In 1998, Datascope created a new subsidiary called Genisphere, which manufactures 3DNA reagents that life sciences researchers use to detect plant, animal, bacterial, and viral genes.

Right: Datascope's Patient Monitoring division headquarters building in Mahwah, New Jersey, is a sleek reflection of the company's dynamic, innovative culture.

As of 2003, Datascope's board consisted of seven of the keenest business minds in the country, including Larry Saper as chairman; Alan Abramson, president of Abramson Brothers, Inc., a real estate firm; David Altschiller, chairman of Altschiller Associates Advertising Agency; William Asmundson, consultant; George Heller, consultant; and Arno Nash, international business consultant.

"We have a first-rate board populated by first-rate minds," said Abramson. "Discussion is open. It's vigorous. It's collegial and respectful. It's a superb board."[67]

Datascope also began replacing its enterprise resource planning (ERP) system, which director of information technology Irv Citrenbaum had implemented in the early 1990s, with a new system by J. D. Edwards. "One World," as it was called, connected every division and department, including the European operations. Because of its complexity, it was still an ongoing project in 2003.

"One World is a centralized system, so we'll have a single computer system supporting our worldwide activities," explained Jeff Skulsky, vice president of information systems. "When it's done, we'll have a high degree of communication and collaboration, something that the divisions really never had in the past."[68]

Skulsky went on to explain some of the benefits of the One World system. "It's more than just J. D. Edwards software, which allows us to invoice," he said. "JDE will provide what we call a data warehouse. It will provide better analytics so we can increase our sales, allow us to see trends, and better establish what our costs are so we can look for opportunities to reduce the cost and create more efficiencies."[69]

In addition, said Gary Sagaas, director of corporate accounting, "We'll be able to close [the fiscal quarters and years] more quickly because we won't have so many people doing so many different things on different systems and then have to convert to the system that puts it all together."[70]

HONORS AND ACCOLADES

For two consecutive years, in 2000 and 2001, Datascope was named one of the 200 Best Small Companies in America by *Forbes* magazine. *Forbes* recognized Datascope for both its long- and short-term performance.

Wall Street gave its own accolades. "We think the company is one of the best values in our universe of medical device stocks and offers significant appreciation potential," said analyst Robert Dunne in early 1999.[71]

In June 2001, Frost & Sullivan, which specializes in international strategic market consulting and training, honored Datascope with its annual Competitive Strategy Award for managing to increase sales of its respiratory gas monitors, despite an overall slowing of the market in 2000. The award was given to companies that showed significant gains in market share. It considered how quickly companies penetrated new markets and how innovative companies' strategies were. Mahpara Qureshi, a Frost & Sullivan industry research analyst, explained why Datascope won the award.

In the highly competitive patient monitoring market, Datascope has continued to outperform its competitors in the portable monitors market. The company has demonstrated a keen understanding of customer needs for standardized monitoring equipment and offers its products at a competitive price.[72]

SMART PLAYS

The American economy had taken a serious beating since the terrorist attacks of September 11, 2001. The Enron debacle and other cases of corporate wrongdoing did nothing to increase investors' confidence, and the economic slump deepened. These conditions, coupled with high oil prices, spiraling healthcare costs, and the impending war on Iraq, kept many businesses from growing as they waited and watched and hoped for good times to return. Businesses both large and small initiated sweeping layoffs, and highly skilled men and women found themselves lining up at unemployment offices and temp agencies as those businesses that hadn't already downsized downshifted into stagnant mode.

Datascope fared better than most. As Saper wrote to shareholders in the 2001 annual report, "While no industry or business will be completely insulated from current economic conditions, we believe the medical industry is likely to be less susceptible than most." These words were written before 9/11, when competition was Datascope's primary concern. By the end of 2001, the company was contending with increased competition and a rapidly crumbling American economy coupled with an uncertain international market, where almost a third of its sales originated.

Datascope had all the right moves. Its reputation for maintaining a healthy balance sheet continued to attract investors and please shareholders. Sales at the end of fiscal 2003 stood at $328.3 million, and net earnings were $23.3 million. To enhance shareholder value, Datascope's board approved several stock repurchase programs, and the company began paying quarterly cash dividends in 1999. "That's the company's way of giving something back to the stockholders," said Marty Nussbaum.[73]

With no debt and plenty of dollars for working capital, Datascope was able to continue reinvesting in research and development to keep its pipeline full of new products. "As a business model, Datascope is as good as it gets," said board member Alan Abramson. "This is a company that has no debt, sits on considerable cash reserves, and is continually plowing money back into research and development to make itself a better company."[74]

"Being conservative means it's easier to gauge the direction we should go," said Ronald Doyle, director of credit. "We take appropriate risks. We're not one to get into some crazy area with respect to accounting or credit practices."[75]

CFO Murray Pitkowsky explained why investors liked Datascope.

They're attracted to our balance sheet. Not only is it debt free; it's very, very strong. They're attracted to our cash flow. The businesses have very high margins to go with our market shares. We are a traditional cash generator. They're impressed with the fact that we're innovative and that we invest in our R&D. They like our margin structure, and finally, they like the fact that we're decisive. When we have to close businesses or have restructuring, they're confident that we're not shy about making decisions that are right for the business. Finally, they're attracted to the fact that we make decisions that are right for the long term.[76]

New products are the lifeblood of many companies, especially those in the highly competitive medical device industry. "Our overriding and constant goal is making our company stronger by always building for future growth," Saper told investors in October 2002. "Our goal is always to drive growth by constantly building a timely pipeline of new products in each of our four businesses. Our goal is to exploit opportunities as they arise."[77]

Indeed, Datascope headed into 2003 with a solid base of existing products and a pipeline of new ones.

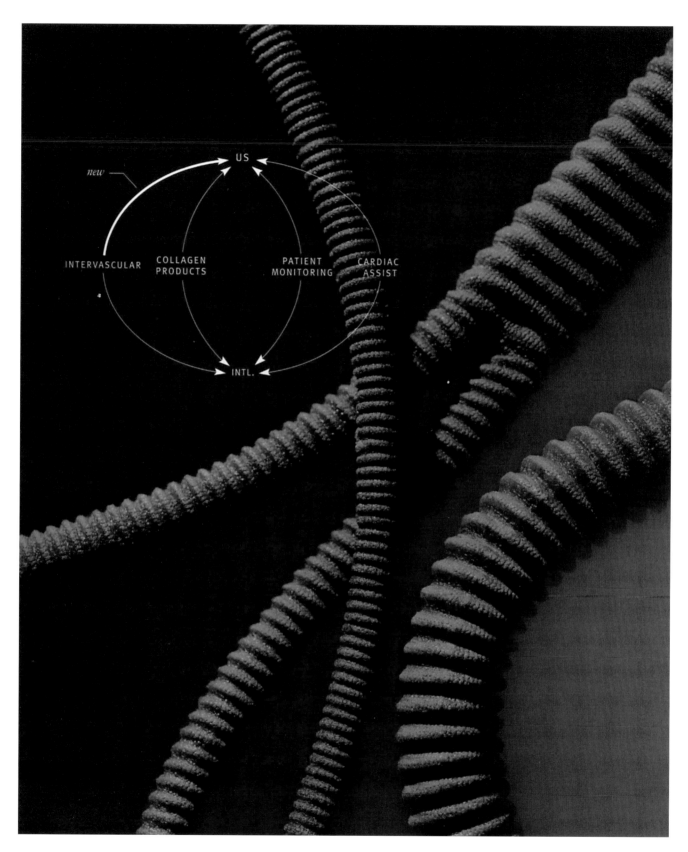

Datascope's InterVascular unit, a market leader in vascular technology, launched its first direct sales organization in the United States in January 2002.

CHAPTER NINE

RAISING THE BAR

2003 AND BEYOND

We are motivated by the opportunity to seek out and solve problems in the medical community.

— Larry Saper, 2002

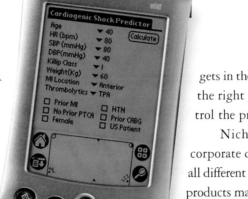

DATASCOPE'S PROCESS FOR creating each new product involved a mixture of innovation, foresight, precision, and teamwork. In many creative companies, only engineers are involved on the ground floor of product development. But after the FDA issued manufacturing controls similar to the European Community's rules, Datascope began implementing design controls that traced all the way back to the product's concept.

The design controls required input from multiple departments, including research and development, engineering, manufacturing, design, quality assurance, marketing, sales, legal, regulatory, and service. "All these people have to sign off," said Frank Casamassina, vice president of manufacturing and quality assurance for Patient Monitoring. "Each function comes with its own perspective on how to look at things."[1]

"Everyone joins together to guide the development of the product to commercialization," said Ari Zak. After all, he said, "There's no sense in spending a year developing a product that somebody else has already patented or that the manufacturing people discover isn't manufacturable."[2]

The key to making the design teams work well, Zak said, was directly related to the people involved. "If the process isn't managed well, it takes on a life of its own and

gets in the way," he said. "You have to have the right people. The people have to control the process rather than vice versa."[3]

Nicholas Barker, vice president of corporate design, said having people from all different departments working together on products made the process smoother. "I don't believe in the 'toss it over the fence' philosophy," he said. "Before I've even started my first sketch, we have marketing people and manufacturing people who share their needs and desires so I can sketch the design to take those into account."[4]

To ensure reliability of the product, the engineers included multiple redundant safety features. "There would have to be large, mulitmode failures for something to go wrong with the product," said Gary Schwartz, a research and development engineer for Cardiac Assist. "The way we design it, different components can fail in different ways and the device will still function."[5]

Engineers also tried to foresee any and every situation a clinician might be faced with. "We're always trying to

Datascope offers software for the Palm™ OS Handheld that helps medical personnel predict the probability of cardiogenic shock in patients.

make our products smaller, faster, and less expensive," said Bob Hamilton, principal engineer for Cardiac Assist. "But I think the most difficult thing is to take into account every possible situation you might experience clinically and address those issues before the product gets out the door."[6]

In addition, Schwartz said, the engineering staff held long meetings to make the product the best it could be. "We go through every painstaking detail where we all sit around and just rip the design apart and try to think of any possible way the individual components can fail, and we take those possibilities and design around them."[7]

Schwartz described how Datascope's inventions moved from the initial sketches to manufacturing.

In the prototype lab we do the concept-to-reality stuff. We take some concepts from the Ph.D.s – the guys that do the inventing – and sometimes these are just napkin sketches. Oftentimes, there's really not much to go on. Then we select the materials and build the first conceptual prototypes. Usually, the first prototypes are show-and-tell pieces for the directors to look at, more of a concept model.

Then, from that model, we turn it into a working device that's suitable for animal testing, and if that's successful, we hand it off to the development group.

The development group takes care of the ISO certification and all the regulatory testing, and they build up the manu-

Datascope is the only company to offer five small intra-aortic balloon catheters designed for children and infants.

facturability of the product, which is important because sometimes it's easy to make six of a product in the lab, but when you need to make 600 a day, things need to change.

Then it goes to manufacturing engineering, where some of the component materials of the product might change to make it easier to manufacture, and when that's finalized, it goes into manufacturing.[8]

Each product also went through rigorous testing. The intra-aortic balloon catheters, for example, were tested for flexibility, fatigue, tension, and elongation. "It can't be too brittle, and it can't be too floppy either," said Frank Frisch, senior manufacturing manager for Cardiac Assist. "The doctor has to be able to push it up to where it needs to be, and that's often through a tortuous artery path. Also, intra-aortic balloons are not like PTCA balloons. A PTCA balloon is used for three or four minutes, and then it's out of the person. Our balloons could be used for days, and they have to be designed for that."[9]

NEW OPPORTUNITIES FOR CARDIAC ASSIST

Datascope's wide-ranging educational resources for IABP professionals include introductory, advanced, and IABP transport programs; materials covering theory, catheter insertion, pump operation, and troubleshooting; an interactive CD-ROM; cardiac assist newsletters, and professional articles relating to IABP therapy. A brochure for the patient called "Balloon Pump Therapy: When Your Heart Needs Help" reassures patients who are about to undergo IABP therapy. In easy-to-understand terms, the brochure explains how the heart works, why the heart may need IABP assistance, and how the therapy works.[10]

"We really sell a therapy more than we sell a product," said Paul Southworth, president of Cardiac Assist. "We're a relatively small company, but we'll train between 15,000 and 20,000 nurses this year [2002] so they can properly run the pumps and properly take care of the patients. We do that at no charge. It's part of what we do in partnership with our institutions."[11]

Datascope also partnered with California-based Medsn, one of the world's leading healthcare e-learning solution providers, to develop interactive, on-line training for physicians. "It's becoming increasingly difficult for physicians to

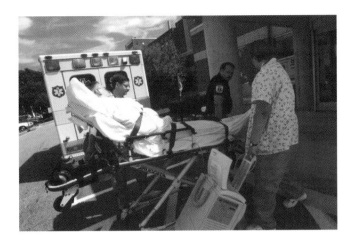

Above: Intra-aortic balloon pumping has proven to increase the chances of survival for cardiogenic shock patients.

Below right: Datascope foresaw IABP therapy being used more often for preoperative support of patients.

attend traditional live meetings," explained Tanya Fawcett, clinical services manager for Cardiac Assist. "That's why we decided to use the Internet to provide e-learning activities. The Medsn modules supplement the traditional live meetings of physicians so that doctors who are too busy to attend symposiums can still benefit from Datascope's education programs." Moreover, physicians who successfully completed the modules earned a continual medical education (CME) certificate, and as Fawcett pointed out, "Physicians have to have so many CMEs per year to renew their licenses."[12]

Though some industry pundits thought Datascope's Cardiac Assist product line was swimming against a mature market and had nowhere else to go, Saper disagreed. "It is a mature market, but there are improvements to be made," he said. "We clearly need and are looking for a second act for Cardiac Assist. And within our company, there are no mature markets, only mature marketing managers."

He went on to explain his vision for the future of IABP therapy.

There has been for some time a feeling and a strong opinion that the therapy of balloon pumping is underutilized both internationally and in the U.S. The first step to increase this was to improve our marketing capabilities. We've done that, and we've improved our sales force capability.

In the future lies the potential for increased application of balloon pumping, which has clear indications for preoperative support for certain patients. Also there is interest in balloon pumping to intervene in the process which occurs when the damage that's inflicted to the heart muscle can't be reversed by doing an acute angioplasty – that is, by opening up the major blood vessel that was obstructed. Rather, the damage has now been found to be caused by damage to the microcirculation, which is not reversed by opening up the flow of blood. Balloon pumping increases blood flow and has been shown to limit the amount of cardiac muscle damage. That would be a stimulus for growth in balloon pumping. It is the simplest and easiest-to-install therapy available for the heart.[13]

To make physicians more aware of the benefits of IABP therapy, the Cardiac Assist division began what Southworth called "indication selling." Until recently, he said, the IABP therapy had sold itself, but "we've reached the point where we've saturated the growth of the market at that level. Now we're focusing on getting the clinical studies and getting the compelling stories to the physician. We're talking to physicians about how we can help them in their practice by using counterpulsation more often to achieve better patient outcomes and quicker turnaround in the hospital. That's where our future growth lies."[14]

Southworth acknowledged that tailoring a sales force for indication selling would be a slow process, but in true

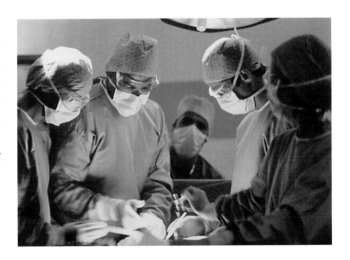

Datascope style, declared, "We're undaunted about the opportunity. We will be successful."[15]

Deb Joseph said Datascope was also looking for opportunities "outside our current sandbox. Right now, all of our indications are within the cardiac/cardiology arena. So we're looking at other opportunities for the therapy — possibly for patients who have suffered a stroke."[16]

Aside from creating new opportunities for IABP therapy, Datascope had several new cardiac assist devices in the pipeline, including a next-generation balloon pump called the CS100 and innovative new catheters. Nicholas Barker explained some of the work that went into the CS100's development.

The CS100 is our first truly automatic pump. Its development drove us to rethink how people will use a new, far more intelligent machine. Much of the user interface had to be completely retooled. This is no small feat on an FDA Class 3, life-sustaining device. It required the repeated and well-documented input of users, clinical experts, designers, and engineers. We are very excited about the results.[17]

And as always, Cardiac Assist's creative team was continually trying to improve the products themselves.

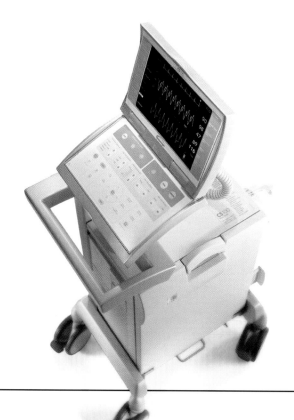

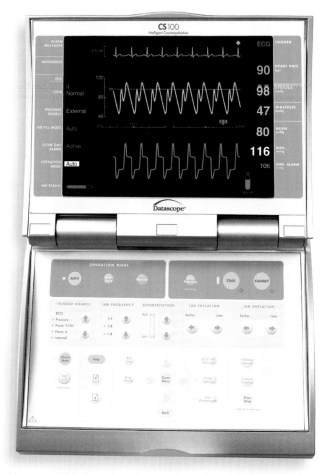

Above and left: Introduced in 2003 and sporting a completely retooled user interface, the CS100 was Datascope's first truly automatic balloon pump.

"When we talk to physicians about why they don't use balloon pumping for patients who really need it, one of their most common answers is, 'It's a lot of trouble to use the technology,'" said Bob Schock, director of advanced research for Cardiac Assist. "We want to help make it easier, so future balloons will be smaller, meaning there will be fewer complications; it will be easier to put in the body. And the pumps will be more automatic in terms of their operation. They'll also give the user more information in terms of monitored functions. Thus, the therapy will become more useful and easier to deliver."[18]

"There's room for breakthroughs in both pumps and balloons," said John Budris, vice president of research and development for Cardiac Assist. "The objective is to make them simpler and easier to use without sacrificing the therapy."[19]

"If the balloon can be smaller, you can insert it through different sites," explained Gary Schwartz. "You don't have to go through the femoral artery. You may be able to go through the radial artery or brachial artery, which would give the patient more mobility. Also, some patients have so much calcium in their arteries that you can't get the balloon through, and if the balloon is smaller, that wouldn't be as much of a problem."[20]

PATIENT MONITORING: OUTDOING THE COMPETITION

Datascope emerged from the 1990s as the recognized world leader in portable monitoring, offering a full line of bedside, stand-alone, and transport monitors with a wealth of supplies and accessories. As Donald Southard, president of Patient Monitoring, observed, Datascope was one of the last independent monitoring companies, competing with multibillion-dollar corporations like Agilent Technologies (owned by Philips Electronics), G.E. Medical Systems, and Datex. "It's quite a testimonial to the company culture that we compete with these behemoths," he said. "Larry has fostered that culture. If it wasn't for him, or if we were managed by a lesser group of individuals, we would have been sold off years ago. Because we've invested heavily in our engineering resources and development efforts, we are the fastest-growing monitoring company within our space in the industry."[21]

Saper explained another reason why Datascope stood head and shoulders above the competition in patient monitoring.

We're a niche player, and we have a terrific mix of good products that stand up against the competition. Also, we've aimed our products toward the growth sector[s], ... which are the surgical surgery centers, the day surgery centers, ... and the

wireless monitoring market. We're also gaining market share in well-established markets.[22]

Datascope was, in fact, well ahead of the competition when it came to seeking opportunities in ambulatory surgical centers (ASCs). The ASC market "represents one of the few unsaturated markets left in patient monitoring," reported American Health Consultants Inc. "This hasn't escaped the notice of several ... monitoring vendors who have focused on this segment and quietly grabbed market shares. . . . The unquestioned leader in the freestanding ASC space is Datascope."[23]

"Picking submarkets within our markets is very important," said Southard. "And we've done a good job of picking parts of the market that have grown: telemetry, portable monitoring, bedside products, and battery-operated monitors."[24]

Despite the fact that the entire patient monitoring industry was only growing at between 1 percent and 3 percent a year, the Patient Monitoring division was growing at a substantially higher rate — from 5 to 10 times faster, according to Southard. Moreover, Patient Monitoring had grown from 25 percent to 30 percent a year in international markets for three consecutive years.

"One reason we're growing faster than the market is because we have a very good understanding of what the customer wants," said Southard. "Our corporate design group spends a lot of time studying how the customer uses the equipment, and then we design our

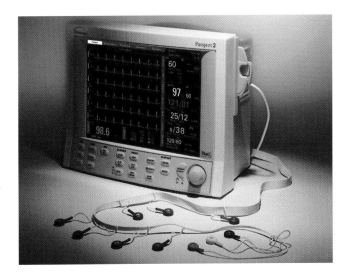

View 12, an accessory to Passport 2, turns every bed into a cardiac bed by giving a picture of patients' hearts before they exhibit symptoms or as they recover. The module is also easy to transport.

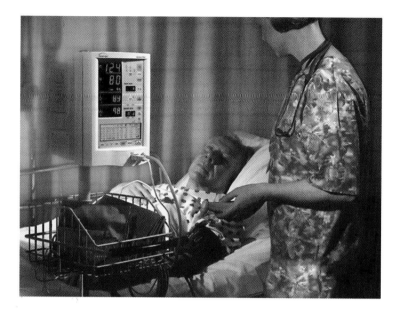

Datascope offers a full line of monitors for hospitals' medical-surgical needs. Like all Datascope monitors, the Accutorr Plus blood pressure module (above and below) is designed for easy use and comes with many options.

products to be very user-intuitive. Customers like that. We have a reputation for listening to them, and we're very good at servicing the equipment we put out in the field."[25]

Datascope's monitors had, in fact, become the industry standard in terms of design and ergonomics. "The designs are terrific," said vice president of business development Tom Dugan. "They're easy to use and provide everything the clinician wants."[26]

Datascope's clinical education specialists helped hospitals effectively utilize all of the monitors' functions so hospitals could provide the best possible patient supervision. The company also offered service programs tailored to individual hospitals and offered emergency loaner and rental programs.

For the future, Patient Monitoring would continue listening to medical professionals and develop innovative technologies designed to address their needs. It would also continue to improve the products' accuracy and efficiency so that medical professionals could focus their efforts, not on running the equipment, but on providing the best possible patient care.

"You can never have too many products coming down the pipeline," said Steve Block, vice president of sales and marketing worldwide for Patient Monitoring. "And we're always challenging what we do. The status quo doesn't mean it's good enough."[27]

One of the products in development in 2003 was a low-cost noninvasive blood pressure (NIBP) monitor called Duo. It would be an extension of Datascope's existing NIBP product line and would offer an LED display, single touch-button user interface, a removable battery, an internal power supply, and optional pulse oximetry and predictive temperature.

"Unlike Trio, Duo won't be used for continuous monitoring," explained Sondra Kaufman, associate business manager for Patient Monitoring. "Duo is a device that you would bring from patient to patient and just check their vital signs on an interval basis. It's kind of the baby brother of Passport 2. There are certain markets that don't require all the features of the Passport 2, and Duo is a lower-cost monitor that satisfies requirements of those markets."[28]

The Patient Monitoring division had other devices in the works, too. "We've got some products in the pipeline that I think are going to be very well accepted in markets we don't play in today," said Southard. "We'll potentially have some technological advantages over our competitors, and that will allow us to continue growing at a pace that's well above the market's growth."[29]

Don Southard predicted that the monitoring market would move toward more wireless communication, and he wanted Datascope to be on the forefront of this trend. "Technology has been developed that would allow any patient in any bed to be attached via a radio frequency product to a network that can communicate patient data to caregivers wherever they may be — at the bedside, at the nurse's station, in the cafeteria, over the Internet in a different department, or through the Internet at their home. The technology is being used in other applications. It's just a matter of being smart enough to figure out how to allow any caregiver across the globe to look at a patient's real-time data."[30]

Above: New for 2003, Safeguard provides an alternative way of managing puncture site wounds after hemostasis.

Below right: Datascope's thrombectomy device, ProLumen, launched in early 2004, helps patients undergoing kidney dialysis. The device breaks up blood clots that form during dialysis, thus restoring the flow of blood so the patient can continue the dialysis uninterrupted.

INTERVENTIONAL PRODUCTS DIVISION: IMPROVING ON INNOVATION

Datascope's Collagen Products division, renamed Interventional Products, had "a whole series of product innovations to exploit the technology we have," said Peter Hinchliffe, president of the division.[31] Hinchliffe had been vice president of research and development for InterVascular and Collagen Products.

One of those products, Safeguard, made its debut in 2003. Safeguard gave healthcare workers an alternative way of managing the puncture site wound after hemostasis. It combined a built-in inflatable bulb and a sterile dressing to put pressure on the wound. The pressure could be adjusted according to the patient's need.

Hinchliffe explained the benefits of Safeguard:

There are different procedures that people use to close the femoral artery. Some people like to sew the artery closed; others like to put collagen outside the artery to have it closed. In the majority of cases, people are using manual compression, which requires the doctor or nurse or clinician to stand next to the patient and press down

on the hole with their fingers for 20 to 40 minutes until it stops bleeding.

With Safeguard, we've developed a low-cost product that has an adhesive backing. It sticks down very similar to an adhesive bandage. It has a balloon integral inside the device that you inflate, and that inflation puts the exact amount of pressure the doctor or nurse would apply so as not to occlude the flow of blood to the foot – just enough pressure to prevent the bleeding.

Unlike some competitive devices, which wrap around the entire patient and are very similar to a C-clamp, the patient can sit up and move around without the device becoming dislodged because it's adhered right to the patient's skin.

Medical professionals have a very limited amount of time, and Safeguard will enable clinicians to move on to the next patient more quickly.[32]

The Interventional Products division was looking to create other innovative products outside the collagen realm. "Our Interventional Products division has more than 100 sales reps in the United States, and their call points are interventional radiology and interventional cardiology," said Hinchliffe. "We've analyzed that market to find out what other innovative products we could bring to those call points that utilize our 100-plus sales reps."[33]

To that end, in 2004 Datascope launched a thrombectomy device called ProLumen. Hinchliffe explained how the device worked.

Many patients on kidney dialysis have a synthetic graft implanted under the skin in the non-dominant forearm. It's a

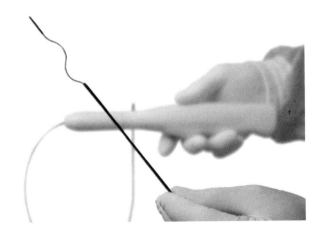

loop graft that gives access for the dialysis machine to the patient's bloodstream. Statistics show that between one and two times per year, this graft will occlude and will have a thrombus build up inside the graft.

Our device is designed to go in through a very small [6 Fr.] sheath and break up the clot and aspirate the clot out before restoring the flow so that the patient can go back to dialysis. It's a totally disposable piece of equipment that is effective, quick, and easy to use.[34]

Also, to ensure that the Interventional Products division didn't get caught flat-footed as it had in the mid-1990s when there were fewer competitors, the R&D team worked with marketing to find out what competitors were doing. R&D also developed relationships with physicians so the company could better anticipate their needs.

Like the other Datascope divisions, Interventional Products provided 24-hour clinical support and a wealth of programs and resources to help customers — both healthcare workers and patients — achieve optimal performance and satisfaction with the product. Datascope was the first medical device company to provide a VasoSeal certification program for physicians. It was also the first to provide formal

competency documentation programs for nurses and technologists. Datascope's consultative services and programs included classes such as "Developing a Hemostasis Teaching Strategy" and "The Standard of Care: VasoSeal VHD." Training and educational materials helped hospitals standardize the use of VasoSeal. Video resources included such titles as "VasoSeal VHD Usage and Technique" and "VasoSeal VHD Post Deployment Patient Care." The company also provided a variety of guides such as "VasoSeal VHD Medical Information Guide," "VasoSeal Patient Information Guide," and "VasoSeal ES Competencies and Skills Check List." Educational resources could also be found on the company's Web site.

INTERVASCULAR: THE START OF SOMETHING BIG

InterVascular's dedication to helping improve clinical outcomes and its willingness to collaborate with vascular and cardiovascular surgeons made it a leader in vascular technology. Though competition in the field remained stiff and the overall market was growing at a snail's pace, John Benkoczy, director of marketing for InterVascular's U.S. operations, noted that InterVascular had only been in the U.S. market since 1997 and still had ample opportunity to expand the business. Moreover, its direct U.S. operations didn't begin until January 2002. "We're like a start-up company," he said, "only we have the backing of a very well established company."[35]

InterVascular planned to gain market share by chipping away at competitors' shares, most of whom held a large portion of the overall market. One way to do that was to develop products that were less invasive, and InterVascular had several less invasive products in development. But Benkoczy said InterVascular was also interested in developing a niche in traditional markets by improving existing products. To do that, InterVascular collaborated with physicians to co-develop new products. It also made sure its products

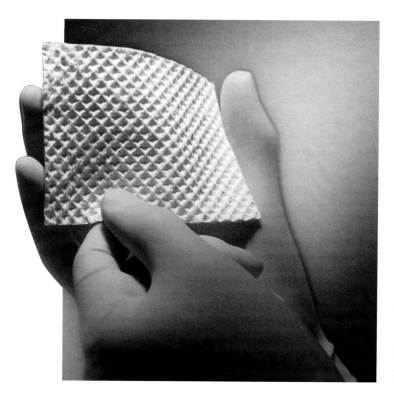

Datascope's FirstStop absorbable collagen hemostat, offered by the Interventional Products division, combines mechanical and biochemical methods to effectively stop bleeding.

InterVascular offers vascular surgeons a complete range of knitted, collagen-coated HemaCarotid Patches in a wide array of sizes. HemaCarotid Patches stop suture bleeding in carotid endarterectomy and angioplasty procedures.

were used in scientific studies that would be published for peer review. "The influence for surgeons to modify or change their techniques is based upon scientific studies that are published in peer review literature," Benkoczy said.[36]

In addition, InterVascular had several development opportunities that could take the division beyond vascular grafts.

A STELLAR REPUTATION

Because Larry Saper was so exacting, because his standards for quality were so high, the Datascope name has long

been equated with excellence, ingenuity, and durability. "There's a certain credibility to products that have the Datascope name on them," said Marty Nussbaum. "Datascope has a real persistence. We're always looking to improve on our products. And we'll work for years to solve a particular [medical] problem. When there's an idea that seems to have merit and the talent to support it, the company takes the time to develop it and do it right."[37]

Barker said the design of the devices was another way to build a trusted brand, noting that all of Datascope's monitors have a unified look. "Our competitors have a hard time doing that right now because they're part of a bigger company," he said. "Sometimes being big when you're trying to control and cultivate a brand identity in product design is not necessarily an advantage."[38]

Datascope also had a reputation for caring, a characteristic the company showed every day through its relationships with physicians, its clinical education, and its 24-hour support and service. But Datascope showed its compassion for people in other ways as well. Lesla Orsino, a licensed nurse and senior business manager in Patient Monitoring, remembered how the Patient Monitoring division rallied to help victims of the September 11, 2001, terrorist attacks. About an hour after the second plane flew into the World Trade Center in New York City, a consortium of hospitals approached Datascope saying they needed monitors and equipment, whatever the company could provide. The company scrambled to assemble as much equipment as it could in a short amount of time. The consortium also needed a qualified person to stay in New York to help service the healthcare workers who would be using the monitors. Orsino volunteered.

"Even though Don Southard had announced we were going to shut down the building out of respect to everybody (since we live so close to New York and many people had relatives or friends who worked in the World Trade Center), most people stayed to help out," Orsino said. "We needed a couple of volunteers from the shipping department to help us load the monitors and equipment, and every person in shipping and manufacturing said they wanted to stay. Don [Southard] was down helping load the monitors; so were the director of finance and the director of sales. Everybody sprung into action. That's the culture at Datascope. Everybody here fosters the 'roll up your sleeves and get it done' attitude."[39]

"I would say uncategorically that this company cares more about its customers and the patients who use our equipment than any of the other six companies I've worked for," said Don Southard. "All of us think that the most important thing is to get a quality, price-performing, value-oriented product out the door as quickly as possible to help the caregiver take care of their patients. We believe the ultimate end user of our products is the patient, and we sell these products based upon making sure that they are products we would like our loved ones to be on if they were in the hospital."[40]

A DEDICATED TEAM

Each of Datascope's four divisions ran autonomously, but they also received support from corporate when needed. "Larry tries to put as few encumbrances on the divisions as possible," said James Cooper, vice president of human resources. "The divisions know they're responsible for running their operations day in and day out, and he makes certain that, as corporate officers, our roles are very hands-on. That's what helps keep us nimble."[41] At the same time, the corporate group ensured that each division had the resources needed to invest in new products and improve its business.

Perhaps Datascope's most distinctive quality was the unusual level of dedication employees had for their jobs.

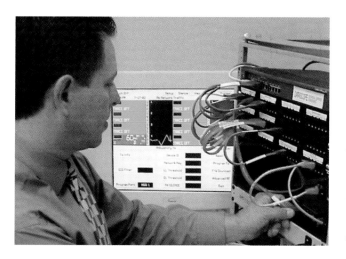

"There's a passion in all the divisions that keeps people there and keeps them striving to do better," said Tanya Fawcett. "It's incredible to see, and I think it's the people who really make this organization the success that it is."[42]

Susan Spadoni, clinical manager for Cardiac Assist, agreed. "What we do is very meaningful, and that's one reason for the longevity of the employees. It's not hard to get excited about making or selling a product or training someone how to use it when that product is going to make a big difference in someone's life."[43]

Mark Rappaport remembered a particularly trying time in December 2000 when the Northeast got hit with the "storm of the century."

It was at the end of the second quarter (and only my second quarter with the company). We'd had a really tough quarter, and we still needed to ship a bunch of product before the end of the quarter. We heard this storm was supposed to blanket us with 30 inches, but we had to get this product shipped. I came in on Saturday morning, and there was a sparse group of people there, including Lisa Brischler, Don Southard, and some of the production and shipping people. Well, it was all hands on deck. All of us, including Don, were on the floor making product all day. Some people tried to come in but were told to stay home because it was a state of emergency in New Jersey. We had to stay in a hotel down the street because we couldn't get home and went right back to it on Sunday morning.

I thought to myself, "This kind of pulling together wouldn't happen at the other places I've been." That weekend was the epitome of what Datascope is all about, and it was after that weekend that the division turned completely around, and we've been growing at double-digit rates ever since.[44]

"People fall in love with this business at a lot of different levels," said Southworth, "but mostly at the center, the feeling that we do good and we help people."[45]

Datascope's support and service network is, according to most sources, the best in the field. Datascope representatives are highly trained and care deeply about their customers — hospitals, surgeons, and especially patients.

All of this translated into a very stable work force. Datascope's Quarter Century Club was made up of employees who had spent at least 25 years with the company. "Bearing in mind that the company is just a little under 40 years old, we still have employees with us who are now attaining the mark of 25 years of service with the company," said Cooper. "We induct a new group of people into the club every year at a luncheon, where we invite back existing members, and Larry personally inducts each new member and congratulates them. He knows many of these folks, and he doesn't get to see them every day, so they both take great delight in having a couple hours of interaction and exchanging stories."[46]

In 2002, the Quarter Century Club had just over 30 members.

THE ENTREPRENEURIAL SPIRIT

Employees of Datascope often commented on the company's entrepreneurialism — its ability to move quickly, the fact that employees had access to senior management, the idea that any employee could use his or her talents to make

Datascope's Quarter Century Club is made up of employees who have spent at least 25 years with the company. In 2002, the Quarter Century Club had just over 30 members.

an impact on the organization, that few boundaries existed when it came to contributing to the company.

Throughout its history, Datascope welcomed challenges as opportunities, and the company had a proven track record of solving medical problems. The string of innovations started with the Carditron, which gave anesthesiologists a better heart monitor. Then Datascope revolutionized counterpulsation therapy with the first commercially produced intra-aortic balloon pump and the first percutaneous balloon catheter. Its research in cardiac assist products led to VasoSeal, the first vascular sealing device. And then the company applied VasoSeal's collagen technology to vascular grafts with InterVascular. In each of these four product segments, Datascope not only pioneered new products but also advanced and improved upon them, becoming a recognizable leader in each of its four product groups.

Though no longer a small company, Datascope managed to keep the dynamic, entrepreneurial spirit alive. "Larry is very consistent in the way he approaches things," said Boris Leschinsky, an inventor who was recruited by Sidney Wolvek in 1990. "When he approaches a new device, he first looks at it from the standpoint of what it is doing for the patient, what kind of problem it solves, how it helps the physician or patient. He is not looking at the financial or regulatory aspects. If, indeed, the potential device would help the patient, he believes the rest of the problems or conditions will take care of themselves. He's always looking for some way to solve a clinical problem, and in that sense, Datascope is an entrepreneurial company."[47]

Saper made a conscious effort to ward off bureaucracy, and the company fostered a culture of bright, motivated people whose shared goal was to improve patient outcomes.

People were not pigeon-holed either, as illustrated by Hank Scaramelli, vice president of finance. At one time Scaramelli stood in as president of Cardiac Assist, but he was involved in many other areas of the company as well. "You can create your own career path," he said. "Most of my time is spent doing whatever I can to help in whatever business, and I enjoy that freedom to get involved in everything. I've even run an R&D project for two years."[48]

Scaramelli was referring to a project still in development called the LifeStick Resuscitator, a device aimed at improving CPR. LifeStick resuscitated the heart by suctioning air from the patient's diaphragm into the chest to get the patient breathing and get the heart pumping. The technique, called interposed abdominal compression CPR, was developed by Dr. David Bregman in the 1980s.

"LifeStick is a work in progress," said Bob Schock. "It's aimed at helping patients who suffer from sudden cardiac arrest. Their heart suddenly stops without warning, even though they're basically healthy people. Basically the patient's brain is salvageable for at least 10 minutes after the heart stops, and if you give CPR, the brain could be salvaged even after one hour of cardiac arrest, but the problem is getting the heart started, getting blood flow established."[49]

LifeStick's design won an international award from the Industrial Design Society of America (IDSA) and was featured in *Business Week* and *Popular Science.*

"There's not a lot of red tape in this organization," said Irv Citenbaum. "So if you have an idea, you can take it and run with it, and generally that's how most people in this company have been successful."[50]

The entrepreneurial spirit started at the top of the organization with Saper and trickled its way down to every employee. Though Saper turned 75 in 2003, his mind was as sharp as a

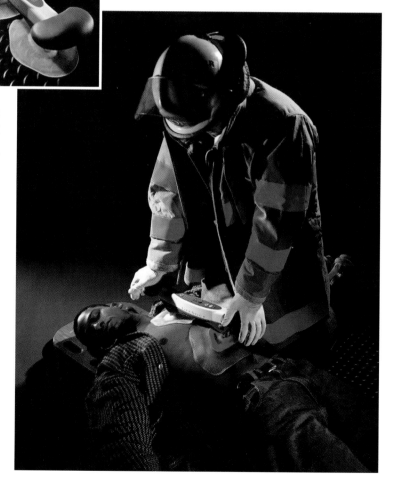

Right and inset: The LifeStick Resuscitator uses interposed abdominal compression CPR to resuscitate the heart.

razor, and he continued working hands-on in the company he created.

"Mr. Saper's working habits haven't changed much in my 28 years with the company," said Susan Chapman. "He's as driven as he's ever been, and he's always been completely hands-on, involved in everything from product literature to service manuals and writing quarterly reports. He stays in touch with doctors to figure out what they need and want, and he's constantly in meetings with engineering and product development."[51]

Saper enjoyed naming new products and took his role as critic of potential products very seriously. "He will test and challenge the decisions that we have made on the user interface of our monitors," said Block. "If he can't figure out how to turn it on and get to the first level of menus within 30 seconds, we know we have a problem."[52]

"Larry is very dynamic," said Murray Pitkowsky. "That's what attracted me to this company. That and the innovation. He's the heartbeat of this company, and his standards are so high that they're tough to meet. When he puts a product out on the market, he doesn't want it to be another me-too product. He wants the best, one that benefits the medical profession and patients."[53]

"Larry is a brilliant man, a lovely human being," said Len Gottlieb, a financial consultant who knew Saper even before he founded Datascope. "He cares about the employees and treats everyone fairly and ethically."[54]

At the same time, Saper never lost the enthusiasm and magnetism that had brought Datascope from the kitchen table to the big leagues.

"The difference between Larry and most people is that he can't wait to get to work," said his wife Carol. "He has a tremendous appetite for it. Every day of his life, he's excited." But unlike many people, Larry Saper didn't let his love of work get in the way of family and life. "That's the other part about Larry," Carol said. "He's so much fun."[55]

All across the company, employees express their respect for Larry Saper. His ingenuity, compassion, and innovative spirit have led Datascope from a one-product company in 1964 to a multimillion-dollar, diversified medical device corporation.

Saper himself remained humble about his accomplishments but set his sights on achieving even greater things, not for his own satisfaction, but to improve the lives of patients and to help physicians and hospitals provide better healthcare. "We prize innovation," he said. "The desire to innovate is a basic element of our company's character.... [We will] work for our future growth with great energy, and for all the right reasons."[56]

A HISTORY OF INNOVATION
DATASCOPE CORP.
1964–2003

1964

After inventing the Carditron — the first portable heart monitor and the first to synchronize the ECG trace with a patient's heart rate — Larry Saper founds Datascope.

1972

Datascope goes public on Nasdaq.

1981

Datascope begins a formal clinical education services department staffed by registered nurses who are experts in critical care.

1965

George Heller joins the company as sales manager, and he and Saper create a marketing, sales, and product plan for both domestic and international growth.

1976

The Medical Device Amendments Act mandates that new medical devices must be approved by the FDA before they can be marketed.

1998

Datascope forms a new subsidiary called Genisphere to manufacture and market 3DNA, which are used to detect and measure other biological substances.

2003

After refocusing its R&D efforts, Datascope enters the future with a pipeline of new, innovative products.

Genisphere®

1990

The company strengthens operations by dividing into divisions.

2000

Datascope is named one of the 200 Best Small Companies in America by *Forbes* magazine, an honor that is repeated the following year.

A HISTORY OF INNOVATION
PATIENT MONITORING

1964–2003

1968

Datascope outdoes itself with the Datascope 850.

1981

Datascope launches an innovative series of automatic noninvasive blood pressure monitors with the Accutorr 1.

1983

The Accucap becomes the next innovation for monitoring patients in the operating room under anesthesia.

1987

The noninvasive Accusat pulse oximeter makes its debut.

1989

Datascope introduces the Flexisensor oximetry sensor system.

1973

The M/D2, a combination monitor/ defibrillator hits the market.

1982

Datascope kicks off the 2000 monitor series for anesthesiologists.

1984

The Accutorr Central system commences shipping.

1988

The Multinex, a groundbreaking respiratory gas monitor, hits the market.

1996

Datascope partners with Masimo Corporation and incorporates Masimo's signal extraction technology, for monitoring pulse oximetry, into its monitors.

2000

PatientNet, a new central station monitor, can monitor up to 16 patients via telemetry.

2003

The portable Trio monitor is designed to meet the constantly changing demands of modern hospital environments.

1992

Datascope introduces Passport, the first portable large-screen bedside monitor.

1998

Gas Module is introduced as a companion to Passport.

2002

Spectrum, ideal for monitoring critical care patients, makes its debut.

1992

The Visa Central Station monitor is introduced. It can be linked to eight Passports via telemetry.

1997

Datascope partners with Fukuda Denshi Company and begins selling Expert, a high-end monitor.

1999

Passport 2, a portable, battery-powered bedside monitor that weighs only 13.9 pounds, revolutionizes patient monitoring.

2002

Datascope enters the anesthesia machine market with Anestar.

A HISTORY OF INNOVATION
CARDIAC ASSIST

1970–2003

1970

Datascope broadens its product line with a portable, battery-powered defibrillator called the Resuscitron.

1971

System 80 becomes the next-generation IABP system.

1981

Patients can now receive IABP therapy while being transported, thanks to Datascope's System 84 transport pump.

1981

Datascope launches the first accredited clinical education program to provide training to physicians, nurses, and technicians on its IABP system.

1986

Datascope begins marketing IABPs that have prefolded membranes. It also unveils the System 90 IABP, which brings counterpulsation therapy to a new level.

1991

Datascope introduces the only intra-aortic balloon catheter specifically designed for sheathless insertion.

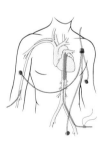

1970

Datascope breaks new ground by creating the first commercial intra-aortic balloon pump (IABP) system, which assists the heart through counterpulsation therapy.

1979

Datascope revolutionizes the IABP market with Percor, the world's first percutaneous intra-aortic balloon catheter.

1984

Datascope introduces the first pediatric-sized balloon catheter.

1987

The System 90T IABP helps hospitals take better advantage of life-saving counterpulsation therapy.

1999

The revolutionary Profile 8 Fr. makes its debut. Profile has the lowest insertion profile of any other adult-sized balloon catheter.

1993

Datascope's System 97 "Small Wonder" IABP incorporates advanced features and is 60 percent smaller than other bedside pumps.

2003

With a completely retooled user interface, the CS100 was Datascope's first truly automatic balloon pump.

1998

The System 97e is introduced to the worldwide market.

2000

The System 98XT uses enhanced software to automatically adapt to irregularities in the patient's heartbeat.

1999

System 98 incorporates faster pneumatics and proprietary algorithms to more effectively time the pumping with the patient's heartbeat.

1992

The System 95 IABP, featuring a built-in computer modem, moves IABP therapy to the next level.

1997

Benchmark, a PC-based database, manages clinical IABP data.

2002

Fidelity becomes the most advanced intra-aortic balloon catheter on the market.

A HISTORY OF INNOVATION

INTERVENTIONAL PRODUCTS

1982–2004

1982

While researching artificial heart valves, Datascope begins looking at other medical applications for collagen.

1984

Datascope begins manufacturing its own creation of collagen designed to control bleeding during surgery.

1991

Datascope announces VasoSeal VHD, the first product to effectively seal arterial puncture wounds from coronary angioplasty and angiography. VasoSeal creates an entirely new market for sealing arterial punctures after catheterization.

1983

Datascope acquires the rights to a new hemostatic collagen fleece and constructs a clinical testing and manufacturing facility in Holland.

1985

Datascope introduces a revolutionary biodegradable hemostatic collagen pad, later called FirstStop.

VasoSeal®

1992

Datascope begins marketing VasoSeal to international markets.

1995

The company gets FDA approval to begin marketing VasoSeal in the United States as a device that reduces the time to hemostasis in angiography and coronary angioplasty and allows immediate removal of the sheath following angioplasty.

1997

Datascope begins marketing VasoSeal's other unique qualities. Patients who receive VasoSeal can be ambulated earlier. It can be used in radiology procedures and in patients receiving stents. It increases patient satisfaction and comfort. And it can be deployed by nurses and technicians.

2002

Datascope introduces new innovations to VasoSeal, including an improved deployment method called Elite Technique; VasoSeal Elite, which significantly reduces time to hemostasis compared to other collagen sealing products; and VasoSeal VHD Low Profile, which is designed to seal punctures made by 4 Fr. and 5 Fr. catheters.

2004

ProLumen will help patients undergoing kidney dialysis. The device breaks up blood clots that form during dialysis, thus restoring the flow of blood so the patient can continue the dialysis uninterrupted.

1996

VasoSeal sees increased sales, despite intense competition. It is better than competitive devices because its sealing is extravascular — i.e., it doesn't leave anything behind in the artery.

1998

VasoSeal ES eliminates the need to measure how deep to insert the VasoSeal device and features a one-size-fits-all design.

2003

Safeguard provides an alternative way of managing puncture site wounds after hemostasis.

A HISTORY OF INNOVATION
INTERVASCULAR
1988–2003

1988

Datascope completes its first acquisition, buying InterVascular, a start-up company founded by Dr. George Goicoechea.

1990

InterVascular opens an office in La Ciotat, France.

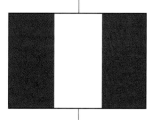

1991

InterVascular begins shipping ULP, a woven, Dacron graft for abdominal and thoracic applications, in the United States.

1988

After applying Datascope's collagen technology to InterVascular's grafts, InterVascular creates Hemaguard and Poly-Graft (later renamed InterGard), collagen-coated vascular grafts that eliminate the need for preclotting. The company begins selling the new grafts to international markets.

1990

InterVascular introduces the Hemaguard RS and Poly-K RS, the first non-Teflon artificial grafts for vessels.

1997

InterVascular significantly increases sales after it begins selling InterGard vascular grafts in the United States and Japan.

1998

The InterGard Heparin graft is introduced in Europe. These grafts reduce the development of blood clots, which are associated with high risk of limb loss.

2000

InterVascular ends operations in Clearwater, Florida, and moves to the newly expanded facility in La Ciotat, France.

2002

Datascope begins selling InterVascular products through its own direct sales force in the United States.

1999

InterGard Silver debuts in Europe. It is the first graft in the world to use an antimicrobial agent (silver) to reduce the chance of infection after the graft is implanted.

2001

InterGard Heparin becomes the first vascular graft that incorporates a drug to be approved by the FDA.

2003

InterVascular begins selling InterGard Silver in the United States.

NOTES TO SOURCES

CHAPTER ONE

1. Adam Saper, *My Father*, video recording, 8 September 1998.
2. Larry Saper, interview by Jeffrey L. Rodengen, tape recording, 4 April 2002, Write Stuff Enterprises.
3. Ibid.
4. Ibid.
5. Ibid.
6. Ibid.
7. Ibid.
8. Ibid.
9. Ibid.
10. Ibid.
11. Ibid.
12. Ibid.
13. Ibid.
14. Ibid.
15. Ibid.
16. Ibid.
17. Ibid.
18. Ibid.

CHAPTER TWO

1. Larry Saper, interview, 4 April 2002.
2. Ibid.
3. Sam Gerson, interview by Richard F. Hubbard, tape recording, 1 October 2002, Write Stuff Enterprises.
4. Larry Saper, interview, 4 April 2002.
5. "This May Well Be the World's Most Advanced ECG Monitor, It is Called the Carditron," Datascope product brochure, 1.
6. Larry Saper, interview, 4 April 2002.
7. Ibid.
8. Ibid.
9. Larry Saper, interview by Jeffrey L. Rodengen, tape recording, 2 June 2002, Write Stuff Enterprises.
10. Larry Saper, interview, 4 April 2002.
11. Ibid.
12. Ibid.
13. Ibid.
14. Ibid.
15. Raymond D. Bahr, M.D., "Chest Pain Centers: Moving Toward Proactive Acute Coronary Care, History of Coronary Care in the United States," Society of Chest Pain Centers, 12 March 1999, http://www. Scpcp.org/library/ proactive/history.html.
16. Stephen Streat, "Coronary Care Units: Background on CCUs, Ministerial Review of Coronary Care Units in Victoria," 3 January 1999, http://medmic02.wnmeds.ac.nz/ groups/rmo/arrest29.html.
17. Bahr, "Chest Pain Centers."
18. Lee H. Monsein, "Primer on Medical Device Regulation, Part I History and Background, RSNA," Regulatory Articles, Radiology 1997; 205:1–9, http://www.rsna.org/REG/ research/monsein1.html.
19. Daniel J. Goldstein, M.D. and Mehmet C. Oz, M.D., *Cardiac Assist Devices,* (Armonk: Futura Publishing, 2000), 5.
20. Larry Saper, interview, 4 April 2002.

21. George Heller, interview by Richard F. Hubbard, tape recording, 8 April 2002, Write Stuff Enterprises.
22. Ibid.
23. Adam Saper, *My Father*.
24. Heller, interview.
25. Ibid.
26. Ibid.
27. Adam Saper, *My Father*.
28. Heller, interview.
29. Larry Saper, interview, 4 April 2002.
30. Joseph Grayzel, interview by Jeffrey L. Rodengen, tape recording, 3 April 2002, Write Stuff Enterprises.
31. Arno Nash, interview by Richard F. Hubbard, tape recording, 1 October 2002, Write Stuff Enterprises.
32. Martin Nussbaum, interview by Richard F. Hubbard, tape recording, 7 October 2002, Write Stuff Enterprises.
33. Larry Saper, interview by Jeffrey L. Rodengen, tape recording, 4 June 2002, Write Stuff Enterprises.
34. Ibid.
35. Ibid.
36. Ibid.
37. Ibid.
38. David Aultschiller, interview by Richard F. Hubbard, tape recording, 26 September 2002, Write Stuff Enterprises.
39. Ibid.
40. Larry Saper, interview, 4 June 2002.
41. Ibid.

42. Datascope 1972 Annual Report, 3.
43. Heller, interview.
44. Tony Muldoon, "Teams of Paramedics Proposed for Bergen," *Bergen County Record*, 1973.
45. Adam Saper, interview by Jeffrey L. Rodengen, tape recording, 4 June 2002, Write Stuff Enterprises.
46. Heller, interview.
47. Datascope 1972 Annual Report, 5.

CHAPTER TWO SIDEBAR

1. Monte M. Poen, *Harry S. Truman Versus the Medical Lobby: The Genesis of Medicare* (London: University of Missouri Press, 1979), 1.

CHAPTER THREE

1. Heller, interview.
2. Spyridon D. Moulopoulos, Stephen Topaz, and Willem J. Kolff, "Diastolic Balloon Pumping (with Carbon Dioxide) in the Aorta—A Mechanical Assistance to the Failing Circulation," *American Heart Journal*, May 1962, 669.
3. Ibid.
4. Ibid.
5. Larry W. Stephenson, M.D., with Jeffrey L. Rodengen, *State of the Heart: The Practical Guide to Your Heart and Heart Surgery*, (Fort Lauderdale: Write Stuff Enterprises, 1999), 185–186.

6. Robert B. Schock, "In Memoriam: Sid Wolvek," *Artificial Organs*, 1998, 353.
7. Larry Saper, interview, 4 June 2002.
8. Heller, interview.
9. Grayzel, interview.
10. Ibid.
11. Larry Saper, interview, 4 June 2002.
12. David Bregman, interview by Richard F. Hubbard, tape recording, 19 September 2002, Write Stuff Enterprises.
13. Ibid.
14. Ibid.
15. Ibid.
16. Ibid.
17. Ibid.
18. Ibid.
19. Ibid.
20. Larry Saper, interview, 4 April 2002.
21. Heller, interview.
22. Larry Saper, interview, 4 June 2002.
23. Heller, interview.
24. Ibid.
25. Datascope 1985 Annual Report, 9.
26. Ibid.
27. Grayzel, interview.
28. Datascope 1972 Annual Report, 4.
29. Heller, interview.
30. Ibid.
31. Stephenson with Rodengen, *State of the Heart*, 185.
32. Larry Saper, interview, 4 June 2002.
33. Datascope 1972 Annual Report, 4.

34. Jeffrey L. Rodengen, *The Ship in the Balloon: The Story of Boston Scientific and the Development of Less-Invasive Medicine* (Fort Lauderdale: Write Stuff Enterprises, 2001), 47.

35. Datascope 1972 Annual Report, 5.

CHAPTER THREE SIDEBAR

1. Paul Southworth, interview by Richard F. Hubbard, tape recording, 3 April 2002, Write Stuff Enterprises.

2. Grayzel, interview.

3. Ibid.

4. Nash, interview.

CHAPTER FOUR

1. George B. Tindall and David E. Shi, *America*, 2nd ed. (New York: W. W. Norton & Company, 1989), 911–912.

2. Ibid.

3. Ibid.

4. "Inflation and Deflation," *Microsoft Encarta 97 Encyclopedia.*

5. Datascope 1972 Annual Report, 4.

6. Nussbaum, interview.

7. Datascope 1972 Annual Report, 2, 4.

8. John Henry, "Mobile Heart Care: A Pulsing Industry," *Newsday*, 13 February 1973.

9. Datascope 1974 Annual Report, 4.

10. Datascope 1975 Annual Report, 4.

11. W. A. Tacker Jr., "Electrical Dose for Defibrillation," Cardiac Defibrillation Conference, Purdue University, October 1975.

12. Datascope 1976 Annual Report, 8; print advertisement for the Datascope M/D2J, 1976.

13. Ibid.

14. Orlo Mohr, *Thurston County Chronicle*, September 1977.

15. Datascope 1978 Annual Report, 3.

16. Mark Rappaport, interview by Richard F. Hubbard, tape recording, 4 June 2002, Write Stuff Enterprises.

17. Datascope 1972 Annual Report, 3.

18. Datascope 1973 Annual Report, 2, 6.

19. Ibid., 6.

20. Datascope 1974 Annual Report, 6.

21. Datascope 1977 Annual Report, 4; print advertisement for the Datascope 870, 1977.

22. Ibid.

23. Datascope 1977 Annual Report, 4.

24. Datascope 1978 Annual Report, 4.

25. Datascope 1977 Annual Report, 4.

26. Datascope 1974 Annual Report, 8.

27. Datascope 1975 Annual Report, 8–9.

28. Datascope 1976 Annual Report, 2.

29. Ibid.; print advertisement for the PAD, 1976.

30. "New Pulsatile Assist Device Reduces Open Heart Surgery Risk," Atlanta, GA, Mid-Meeting Issue, vol.2, no. 2, October 24–28, 1976.

31. Datascope 1978 Annual Report, 2.

32. Ibid., 7.

33. Datascope 1972 Annual Report, 4.

34. Ibid.

35. Datascope 1975 Annual Report, 2.

36. Heller, interview.

37. Warren Shoop, interview by Richard F. Hubbard, tape recording, 4 April 2002, Write Stuff Enterprises.

38. Rappaport, interview.

39. Heller, interview.

40. Shoop, interview.

41. Bob Velebir, interview by Richard F. Hubbard, tape recording, 11 September 2002, Write Stuff Enterprises.

42. Datascope 1974 Annual Report, 3.

43. Datascope 1973 Annual Report, 2.

44. Datascope 1977 Annual Report, 3.

45. Monsein, "History of Medical Device Regulation."

46. Larry Saper, interview by Jeffrey L. Rodengen, tape recording, 31 January 2003, Write Stuff Enterprises.

47. Gary Mohr, interview by Jeffrey L. Rodengen, tape recording, 3 April 2002, Write Stuff Enterprises.

48. Ibid.

49. Ibid.

50. Datascope 1976 Annual Report, 3.
51. Larry Saper, interview, 31 January 2003.
52. Susan Chapman, interview by Jeffrey L. Rodengen, tape recording, 4 June 2002, Write Stuff Enterprises.
53. Ibid.
54. Ibid.
55. Shoop, interview.
56. Bob Hamilton, interview by Richard F. Hubbard, tape recording, 12 September 2002, Write Stuff Enterprises.
57. Rappaport, interview.
58. Ibid.
59. Ibid.
60. Fred Adelman, interview by Jeffrey L. Rodengen, tape recording, 3 April 2002, Write Stuff Enterprises.
61. Rappaport, interview.
62. Datascope 1979 Annual Report, 3.
63. Grayzel, interview.
64. Larry Saper, interview, 31 January 2003.
65. Datascope 1985 Annual Report, 11.
66. Kevin McKean, "Life-Saving Boost for Heart Patients," Associated Press, 28 September 1980.
67. Schock, "In Memoriam: Sid Wolvek."
68. Datascope 1985 Annual Report, 10.
69. McKean, "Life-Saving Boost for Heart Patients."
70. Datascope 1979 Annual Report, 3.

71. Bob Schock, interview by Richard F. Hubbard, tape recording, 4 June 2002, Write Stuff Enterprises.
72. Datascope 1979 Annual Report, 2–3.
73. Heller, interview.
74. Betty Clark, interview by Richard F. Hubbard, tape recording, 4 June 2002, Write Stuff Enterprises.
75. Grayzel, interview.

CHAPTER FOUR SIDEBAR

1. Monsein, "Primer on Medical Device Regulation."

CHAPTER FIVE

1. Ina May Gaskin, "Editorial: Insurance Industry Kills Health Care Reform," *The Farm*, Tennessee, 1994.
2. Adrienne J. Kohls and Jill E. Sherman, "The Quality Movement in Health Care," The Johns Hopkins University School of Public Health, Population Information Program, Baltimore, MD, November 1998.
3. Datascope 1985 Annual Report, 11.
4. Grayzel, interview.
5. Nussbaum, interview.
6. Datascope 1980 Annual Report, 3.
7. Cynthia Wallace, "Details of Rate-setting Mechanism Still Fuzzy," *Modern Healthcare*, May 1983.

8. Ibid.
9. Datascope 1980 Annual Report, 7.
10. Ibid., 8.
11. Datascope 1981 Annual Report, 8.
12. Datascope 1985 Annual Report, 13.
13. Larry Saper, interview, 4 June 2002.
14. Grayzel, interview.
15. Datascope 1982 Annual Report, 3.
16. Datascope 1981 Annual Report, 2.
17. Ibid., 6.
18. Datascope 1982 Annual Report, 8.
19. Ibid.
20. Ibid., 10.
21. Ruth Mason, "Plastic Balloon Saves Her Life," *Daily Journal*, 18 June 1984.
22. Datascope 1983 Annual Report, 6.
23. Frank Frisch, interview by Richard F. Hubbard, tape recording, 11 September 2002, Write Stuff Enterprises.
24. Ibid.
25. Linda Herskowitz, "Test Device Lets Infant's Heart Heal," *Philadelphia Inquirer*, 6 February 1985.
26. Datascope 1984 Annual Report, 4.
27. Frisch, interview.
28. Ibid.
29. Goldstein and Oz, *Cardiac Assist Devices*, 295.
30. Herskowitz, "Test Device Lets Infant's Heart Heal."

31. Datascope 1985 Annual Report, 12.
32. Herskowitz, "Test Device Lets Infant's Heart Heal."
33. Rappaport, interview.
34. Bob Terranova, interview by Richard F. Hubbard, tape recording, 4 June 2002, Write Stuff Enterprises.
35. Datascope 1981 Annual Report, 7.
36. Datascope 1982 Annual Report, 2.
37. Ibid., 6.
38. Datascope 1983 Annual Report, 4.
39. Datascope 1984 Annual Report, 4.
40. Ibid., 7.
41. Ibid., 9.
42. Ibid.
43. Ibid., 4.
44. Jeffrey Cane, "Small Business in Brief," *The Record*, 16 October 1985.
45. Datascope 1985 Annual Report, 13.
46. Datascope press release, PR Newswire, 9 October 1985.
47. John A. Jones, "Datascope Has High Hopes for New Heart Monitor System," *Investor's Daily*, 24 April 1986.
48. Datascope 1985 Annual Report, 13.
49. Adelman, interview.
50. Carol Agnese, interview by Richard F. Hubbard, tape recording, 3 April 2002, Write Stuff Enterprises.
51. Kathy Sizemore, "Profit Gains Provide the Beat at Datascope," *Crain's New York Business*, 12 May 1986.

CHAPTER SIX

1. *CEO Interviews* 11, no. 7, 14 November 1988.
2. Ibid.
3. Datascope press release, PR Newswire, 26 January 1982.
4. Ibid.
5. Datascope 1983 Annual Report, 8.
6. Patrice Napoda, interview by Richard F. Hubbard, tape recording, 11 September 2002, Write Stuff Enterprises.
7. Datascope 1983 Annual Report, 8.
8. Napoda, interview.
9. Datascope 1986 Annual Report, 5–6.
10. Ibid., 3.
11. Datascope 1987 Annual Report, 2.
12. Datascope 1989 Annual Report, 9.
13. Datascope 1986 Annual Report, 7, 8.
14. Datascope 1988 Annual Report, 4.
15. Nussbaum, interview.
16. Datascope 1988 Annual Report, 5.
17. Ibid.
18. Ibid.
19. Larry Saper, interview, 31 January 2003.
20. Datascope 1988 Annual Report, 15.
21. Datascope 1990 Annual Report, 2–3.
22. Datascope 1988 Annual Report, 15.
23. Datascope 1989 Annual Report, 5.
24. Datascope 1990 Annual Report, 3.
25. *CEO Interviews*.
26. Elizabeth Liorente, "A Breath of Fresh Air in Heart Attack Care," *Bergen Record*, 13 August 1989.
27. Ibid.
28. Velebir, interview.
29. Ibid.
30. Datascope 1985 Annual Report, 4.
31. Walter Kaiser, interview by Richard F. Hubbard, tape recording, 27 September 2002, Write Stuff Enterprises.
32. Datascope 1987 Annual Report, 3.
33. Frisch, interview.
34. Ibid.
35. Datascope 1987 Annual Report, 5.
36. Rodengen, *The Ship in the Balloon*, 55–66.
37. Datascope 1987 Annual Report, 7.
38. Ibid., 8.
39. Ibid.
40. Ibid., 7.
41. Ibid., 4, 9.
42. Datascope 1989 Annual Report, 3.
43. Ibid.
44. Mariola B. Haggar, *Investors News*, December 1990.
45. Datascope Angioplasty marketing material, 1990.
46. Ibid.
47. Datascope 1990 Annual Report, 2.

48. Haggar, *Investors News*.

49. *CEO Interviews*.

50. Terranova, interview.

51. Datascope 1986 Annual Report, 3.

52. Datascope 1987 Annual Report, 3; Datascope 1989 Annual Report, 5.

53. Datascope 1988 Annual Report, 3.

54. Annabel Kanabus and Jenni Fredricksson, "History of Aids 1987–1992," Avert.org, http://avert.org/his87_92.htm.

55. Larry Saper, interview, 31 January 2003.

56. *CEO Interviews*.

57. "Bargains of the Big Board," *Fortune*, 22 December 1986.

58. "Datascope Has High Hopes."

59. Theresa Agovino, "Medical Company Gets Some Bedside Comfort," *Crain's New York Business*, 8 May 1989.

60. Larry Saper, interview, 31 January 2003.

61. Datascope 1988 Annual Report, 2.

62. Bill Sternberg, "Medical Products Maker Fit as a Fiddle," *Crain's New York Business*, 1988.

63. Dorothy Hinchcliff, "3 Medical Firms Among 100 That May Grow in Price," *Ashbur Park Press*, 15 August 1988.

64. Agovino, "Medical Company Gets Some Bedside Comfort."

65. "A N.Y. Portfolio: Hot Firms to Watch," *Crain's New York Business*, 16 January 1989.

66. Adelman, interview.

67. Gary Sagaas, interview by Richard F. Hubbard, tape recording, 3 April 2002, Write Stuff Enterprises.

68. Adelman, interview.

69. Patrick McGeehan, "Producing Changes on the Shop," *The Record*, Section B, 23 April 1989.

70. "Jersey Firm Given Nursing Award," PR Newswire, 15 May 1989.

71. Nomination Letter, Academy of Medical Arts and Sciences, Dallas, TX, 3 May 1989.

72. Therese Dudek, interview by Richard F. Hubbard, tape recording, 7 October 2002, Write Stuff Enterprises.

73. Murray Pitkowsky, interview by Jeffrey L. Rodengen, tape recording, 3 April 2002, Write Stuff Enterprises.

74. Larry Saper, interview, 31 January 2003.

75. Lisa Brischler, interview by Richard F. Hubbard, tape recording, 4 June 2002, Write Stuff Enterprises.

76. Gayle Carr, interview by Richard F. Hubbard, tape recording, 4 June 2002, Write Stuff Enterprises.

77. Adelman, interview.

CHAPTER SEVEN

1. Shirley A. Lazo, "Speaking of Dividends," *Barron's*, 2 December 1991.

2. Datascope 1992 Annual Report, 2.

3. Datascope marketing material, 1991.

4. Datascope 1992 Annual Report, 5.

5. Datascope 1994 Annual Report, 6.

6. Nicholas Barker, interview by Jeffrey L. Rodengen, tape recording, 3 April 2002, Write Stuff Enterprises.

7. Ibid.

8. Ibid.

9. Ibid.

10. Frank Casamassina, interview by Richard F. Hubbard, tape recording, 4 April 2002, Write Stuff Enterprises.

11. Information provided by Debra Joseph to Melody Maysonet, June 2003.

12. Datascope 1994 Annual Report, 5.

13. Terranova, interview.

14. Datascope 1992 Annual Report, 6.

15. Ibid.

16. Steve Block, interview by Richard F. Hubbard, tape recording, 4 April 2002, Write Stuff Enterprises.

17. Datascope 1992 Annual Report, 6.

18. Datascope 1993 Annual Report, 4.

19. Datascope 1992 Annual Report, 6.

20. Datascope 1991 Annual Report, 2.

21. Ibid.

22. Roseanne Terraciano, interview by Richard F. Hubbard, tape recording, 3 April 2002, Write Stuff Enterprises.

23. Tim Shannon, interview by Richard F. Hubbard, tape recording, 4 April 2002, Write Stuff Enterprises.
24. Datascope 1995 Annual Report, 7, 9.
25. Terraciano, interview.
26. "Corporate Profile," September 1992.
27. Ibid.
28. Datascope 1991 Annual Report, 4.
29. Lance Ignon, "A Weak Medical Sector Sinks Nasdaq," *Investor's Daily*, 30 April 1991.
30. Roger Lowenstein, "Heard on the Street," *Wall Street Journal*, 11 July 1991.
31. Ibid.
32. Ibid.
33. Patrick McGeehan, "Datascope Reaping Gains of Stock Run-Up," *The Record*, 26 November 1991.
34. Datascope 1992 Annual Report, 4.
35. Ibid., 3; Datascope 1993 Annual Report, 3.
36. Datascope 1994 Annual Report, 3.
37. Ibid., 3–4.
38. "FDA Has Questions About VasoSeal," *Medical Materials Update*, August 1994.
39. Datascope 1995 Annual Report, 7.
40. "Datascope Launches VasoSeal At AHA," PR Newswire, 13 November 1995.
41. Arieh Zak, interview by Jeffrey L. Rodengen, tape recording, 4 June 2002, Write Stuff Enterprises.

42. Larry Saper, interview, 31 January 2003.
43. Datascope 1995 Annual Report, 2.
44. Pitkowsky, interview.
45. Dottie Hanratty, interview by Richard F. Hubbard, tape recording, 11 September 2002, Write Stuff Enterprises.
46. Tom Dugan, interview by Jeffrey L. Rodengen, tape recording, 3 April 2002, Write Stuff Enterprises.
47. Grayzel, interview.
48. Tanya Fawcett, interview by Richard F. Hubbard, tape recording, 25 September 2002, Write Stuff Enterprises.
49. Susan Spadoni, interview by Richard F. Hubbard, tape recording, 25 September 2002, Write Stuff Enterprises.
50. Gordon Dewhurst, interview by Richard F. Hubbard, tape recording, 26 September 2002, Write Stuff Enterprises.
51. Debra Joseph, interview by Richard F. Hubbard, tape recording, 3 April 2002, Write Stuff Enterprises.
52. Ibid.
53. Hanratty, interview.
54. Shoop, interview.
55. Ibid.
56. Ibid.
57. John Benkoczy, interview by Richard F. Hubbard, tape recording, 3 April 2002, Write Stuff Enterprises.
58. Barker, interview.
59. Chapman, interview.

60. Rappaport, interview.
61. Heller, interview.
62. Ibid.

CHAPTER EIGHT

1. Susan Page, "Budget Bill Skirts Some Hard Issues," *USA Today*, 30 July 1997.
2. Arthur Gasch, "Fukuda Denshi Breathes Life into Datascope with New Marketing Alliance," *BBI Newsletter*, December 1997.
3. Datascope 1996 Annual Report, 5.
4. Ibid., 7.
5. Datascope 1997 Annual Report, 4.
6. Ibid., 5.
7. Joseph, interview.
8. Datascope 1999 Annual Report, 9.
9. "Datascope Gets Approval of Balloon Pump and Catheter in Japan," *Biotech Equipment Update*, April 1999.
10. Gary Schwartz, interview by Jeffrey L. Rodengen, tape recording, 4 June 2002, Write Stuff Enterprises.
11. Datascope 2000 Annual Report, 5.
12. Ibid.
13. Datascope 2001 Annual Report, 5–7.
14. Datascope brochure, 2002.
15. Schwartz, interview.
16. Datascope 1996 Annual Report, 8–9.
17. "First Independent Study Comparing Masimo SET to Tyco-Nellcor N595 Presented

at Society for Technology in Anesthesia," PR Newswire, 13 January 2003.

18. Datascope 1996 Annual Report, 8.

19. "Datascope Corp. and Masimo Corp. Announced Expanded Licensing Agreement," Datascope press release, 19 February 1998.

20. Gasch, "Fukuda Denshi Breathes New Life into Datascope."

21. Datascope 1997 Annual Report, 7.

22. "Passport 2: The First Monitor That Asks Less of You," datascope.com, February 2003.

23. Datascope 2000 Annual Report, 7.

24. Datascope 2001 Annual Report, 11.

25. "Q1 2003 Datascope Earnings Conference Call," CCBN, Inc., 24 October 2002.

26. Datascope 2002 Annual Report, 9.

27. ViewPoint product brochure.

28. "Spectrum, Performance and Power," datascope.com, February 2003.

29. Sondra Kaufman, interview by Richard F. Hubbard, tape recording, 20 June 2003, Write Stuff Enterprises.

30. Datascope 1997 Annual Report, 16.

31. Datascope 2001 Annual Report, 20.

32. "Datascope Receives FDA Approval to Sell Second

Generation VasoSeal in the United States," Datascope press release, 23 December 1998.

33. "Datascope Can Widen Sales of Heart Device," The Record, 1 May 1997.

34. Datascope 1997 Annual Report, 9–10.

35. datascope.com, March 2003.

36. "Datascope Gains FDA Nod for Second Wound Sealant," Medical Industry Today, 28 December 1998.

37. Terraciano, interview.

38. "Physician Endorsements," datascope.com, March 2003.

39. Ibid.

40. Datascope 1999 Annual Report, 7.

41. "Physician Endorsements."

42. Datascope 2000 Annual Report, 11.

43. Datascope 1999 Annual Report, 7.

44. Jeffrey Purvin, interview by Richard F. Hubbard, tape recording, 4 April 2002, Write Stuff Enterprises.

45. Ibid.

46. Shannon, interview.

47. Datascope 2002 Annual Report, 12–13.

48. "Abstract of 2002 Year-end Datascope Conference Call," 25 July 2002.

49. "New VasoSeal Elite," product brochure.

50. Terraciano, interview.

51. Benkoczy, interview.

52. "FDA Approves InterGard Heparin Vascular Graft," Datascope press release, 17 January 2001.

53. Brett Giffin, interview by Jeffrey L. Rodengen, tape recording, 3 April 2002, Write Stuff Enterprises.

54. "InterVascular Introduces InterGard Silver in Europe, the First Commercially Available Antimicrobial Vascular Graft," datascope.com, March 2003.

55. Datascope 1999 Annual Report, 11.

56. Datascope 2001 Annual Report, 14.

57. Teruhisa Kazui, M.D., Katsushi Yamashita, M.D., et al., "Use of Aortic Arch Branched Graft in the Treatment of Aortic Arch Aneurysm or Aortic Dissection," datascope.com, March 2003.

58. Anne Cuny, interview by Jeffrey L. Rodengen, tape recording, 3 April 2002, Write Stuff Enterprises.

59. James Cooper, interview by Jeffrey L. Rodengen, tape recording, 4 April 2002, Write Stuff Enterprises.

60. "Q1 2003 Datascope Earnings Conference Call."

61. Giffin, interview.

62. Ibid.

63. Adam Saper, interview.

64. "Datascope Plans to Enter Life Science Research Market," AIDS Weekly, 3 November 1997.

65. 3DNA product brochure, 2002.

66. Datascope 1998 Annual Report, 10.

67. Alan Abramson, interview by Jeffrey L. Rodengen, tape recording, 24 September 2002, Write Stuff Enterprises.

68. Jeff Skulsky, interview by Jeffrey L. Rodengen, tape recording, 3 April 2002, Write Stuff Enterprises.

69. Ibid.

70. Sagaas, interview.

71. David Shook, "Medical Device Maker to Build in Mahwah," *The Record*, 2 February 1999.

72. "Datascope Honored with Competitive Strategy Award from Frost & Sullivan for Respiratory Gas Monitoring Equipment Market."

73. Nussbaum, interview.

74. Abramson, interview.

75. Ronald Doyle, interview by Jeffrey L. Rodengen, tape recording, 4 April 2002, Write Stuff Enterprises.

76. Leonard Goodman, interview by Jeffrey L. Rodengen, tape recording, 4 June 2002, Write Stuff Enterprises.

77. "Q1 2003 Datascope Earnings Conference Call."

**CHAPTER EIGHT SIDEBAR:
SIDNEY WOLVEK:
A LEGENDARY MAN**

1. Schock, "In Memoriam: Sid Wolvek."

2. Gary Schwartz, letter to Jeffrey L. Rodengen, 6 June 2002.

3. Kaiser, interview.

4. Schock, "In Memoriam: Sid Wolvek."

**CHAPTER EIGHT SIDEBAR:
THE REGULATORY PROCESS**

1. Zak, interview.

2. Milton G. Allimadi, "EC Quality Code Sparks U.S. Confusion," *Journal of Commerce*, 15 September 1992.

3. Ibid.

4. Napoda, interview.

5. Mohr, interview.

6. Zak, interview.

7. Ibid.

8. Ibid.

9. Mark Metherell, "Rising Costs Prompt Healthcare Overhaul," *SMH*, 10 October 2002.

10. U.S. Food and Drug Administration, "FDA Launches Initiative to Improve the Development and Availability of Innovative Medical Products," *FDA News*, 31 January 2003.

11. Datascope 2002 Annual Report, 2.

CHAPTER NINE

1. Casamassina, interview.

2. Zak, interview.

3. Ibid.

4. Barker, interview.

5. Schwartz, interview.

6. Hamilton, interview.

7. Schwartz, interview.

8. Ibid.

9. Frisch, interview.

10. datascope.com, January 2003.

11. Southworth, interview.

12. Fawcett, interview.

13. "Abstract of 2002 Year-end Datascope Conference Call," 25 July 2002.

14. Southworth, interview.

15. Ibid.

16. Joseph, interview.

17. Information provided by Nicholas Barker, May 2002.

18. Schock, interview.

19. John Burdis, interview by Richard F. Hubbard, tape recording, 3 April 2002, Write Stuff Enterprises.

20. Schwartz, interview.

21. Donald Southard, interview by Richard F. Hubbard, tape recording, 20 September 2002, Write Stuff Enterprises.

22. "Q1 2003 Datascope Earnings Conference Call."

23. Arthur Gasch, "Opportunities Exist in Ambulatory Surgical Monitoring Market," *BBI Newsletter*, 1 September 2002.

24. Southard, interview.

25. Ibid.

26. Dugan, interview.

27. Block, interview.

28. Kaufman, interview.

29. Southard, interview.

30. Ibid.

31. Purvin, interview.

32. Peter Hinchliffe, interview by Richard F. Hubbard, tape recording, 26 June 2003, Write Stuff Enterprises.

33. Ibid.

34. Ibid.

35. John Benkoczy, interview by Richard F. Hubbard, tape recording, 3 April 2002, Write Stuff Enterprises.

36. Ibid.
37. Hinchliffe, interview.
38. Nussbaum, interview.
39. Lesla Orsino, interview by Richard F. Hubbard, tape recording, 27 June 2003, Write Stuff Enterprises.
40. Southard, interview.
41. Cooper, interview.
42. Fawcett, interview.
43. Spadoni, interview.
44. Rappaport, interview.
45. Southworth, interview.
46. Cooper, interview.
47. Boris Leschinsky, interview by Richard F. Hubbard, tape recording, 12 September 2002, Write Stuff Enterprises.
48. Hank Scaramelli, interview by Jeffrey L. Rodengen, tape recording, 4 April 2002, Write Stuff Enterprises.
49. Schock, interview.
50. Irv Citenbaum, interview by Jeffrey L. Rodengen, tape recording, 4 June 2002, Write Stuff Enterprises.
51. Chapman, interview.
52. Block, interview.
53. Pitkowsky, interview.
54. Len Gottlieb, interview by Richard F. Hubbard, tape recording, 25 November 2002, Write Stuff Enterprises.
55. Carol Saper, interview by Richard F. Hubbard, tape recording, 18 October 2002, Write Stuff Enterprises.
56. Datascope 2002 Annual Report, 2, 7.

INDEX

Page numbers in italics indicate photographs.

intra-aortic balloon pumping system
(IABP) *(Cont'd)*
marketing/sales, 36–37, 58–59,
96–97, 115
Medical Society of the State of
New York award, *36*
Pulsatile Assist Device (PAD),
44, *45*
research and development, 48, 70
training, 44, 55–56, 89, 90, 114
See also balloon catheters;
catheters
inventory efficiency plan
Just In Time (JIT), 77–78
Investor's Daily, 65, 75
Investors News, 73
ISO 9001 certification, 106

J-K-L

JAMA. *See Journal of the American
Medical Association*
Janzen, Ernst, 36, 37, 48, *53*, 56, *76*,
84, 85
Japan, 47, 53, 87, 106
John Hopkins Hospital, 69
Johnson, Lyndon B., 22
Joseph, Debra, 78, 83, 90, 94, 116
*Journal of the American Medical
Association*, *32*

Kaiser, Walter, 70, 95
Kantrowitz, Adrian, 32, 52, 95
Kantrowitz, Arthur, 32
Katzen, Barry, 102
Kaufman, Sondra, 101, 118
Kennedy, Ted, 49
Kolff, J. Willem, 31–32, 34
Koop, C. Everett, 74

La Ciotat, France, 70, 89, 107
Laskey, Richard, 48
Leone, Kathleen, 69

Leschinsky, Boris, 124
Levy, Stuart, 49, 51, 77
LifeStick Resuscitator, *124*
Los Angeles County Fire
Department's Emergency
Rescue Program, 40
Lyndon Johnson's Great Society, 15, 22
Lyng, Ralph, 56

M-N-O

magnetic recording, 15
Mahoney, Matt, 27, 33, 48
Mahwah, New Jersey, 109
Marino, Peter, 76
Masimo Corporation, 98
Masimo SET pulse oximetry, *98*, 99,
101
McDonagh, Bernard, 76
McNerney, Sean, 105, 108
M.D. Buyline, 78
M/D defibrillator series, 38, 40, *41*,
42, *57*, 58
Medical Device Amendments of
1976, 48, 49, 50
Medical Industry Today, 102
Medical Society of the State of New
York, 19–20, 21, 22, 36
Medicare, 15–16, 22, 56–57, 81, 93,
107
Medsn, 114–115
Meister, William, *76*
Micross, 73
MicroStream CO_2, 99
Middle East, 47
Miller, Leslie W., 72
Model 650, 21, 22
Model 790 Recorder, 41
Model 800, 42
Model P, 27
modulation, 14–15
Mohr, Gary, 50, 106
Monastersky, Richard, 89

monitors. *See* Patient Monitoring
division
Monitron, *21*
Montreal Heart Institute, 73
Montvale, New Jersey, *76*, *78*, 89
Morris, Douglas, 73
Moulopoulos, Spyridon, 31–32, 34
Multinex, *74*, 99

Napoda, Patrice, 68, 106
Nasdaq, 39, 86
Nash, Arno, 26, 33, 110
National Heart Institute (NHI), 23
National Institute of Health (NIH),
33, 36
Netherlands, 109
New Court Securities, 26
New York Hospital-Cornell Medical
Center, 32–33
New York Times, 23
NHI. *See* National Heart Institute
NIBP. *See* noninvasive blood pressure
monitor
NIH. *See* National Institute of Health
Nilsen, Thor, 109
1980 Olympic Winter Games, 57
1981 Economic Recovery Tax Act,
67
noninvasive blood pressure monitors
(NIBP), 62–65, *74*, 99, 118
North Shore Hospital, 34
Novacol, 68
Nussbaum, Martin, 26, 39, 55, 69,
111, 121

Oakland, New Jersey, 47, 49, 56,
88, 109
OPEC. *See* Organization of
Petroleum Exporting
Countries
Organization of Petroleum
Exporting Countries
(OPEC), 39